DISCIPLINARY
LITERACY

DISCIPLINARY LITERACY

Redefining Deep Understanding
and Leadership
for 21st-Century Demands

Dr. Thomasina Piercy and Dr. William Piercy

LEAD+
LEARN
PRESS

ENGLEWOOD, COLORADO

The Leadership and Learning Center
317 Inverness Way South, Suite 150
Englewood, Colorado 80112
Phone 1.866.399.6019 | Fax 303.504.9417
www.LeadandLearn.com

Published by Lead + Learn Press, a division of Advanced Learning Centers, Inc.

Funky Tree cover art by Brittney Wilson of Canvas and Cocktails. Used with permission.

Library of Congress Cataloging-in-Publication Data

Piercy, Thomasina DePinto, 1950-
   Disciplinary literacy : redefining deep understanding and leadership for 21st-century demands / Thomasina Piercy and William Piercy.
      p. cm.
   Includes bibliographical references and index.
   ISBN 978-1-935588-06-1 (alk. paper)
   1. Reading (Secondary) 2. Reading comprehension. 3. Content area reading. I. Piercy, William. II. Title.
      LB1632.P52 2011
      428.4071'2--dc22
                                                                2010051783

ISBN 978-1-935588-06-1

Printed in the United States of America

15 14 13 12 11   01 02 03 04 05 06 07

Contents

List of Exhibits

About the Authors

Thomasina D. Piercy, Ph.D., earned her degree in curriculum and instruction with a focus on reading from the University of Maryland. As a principal and a teacher, she taught graduate writing and reading courses to educators from various states in the east coast region. Dr. Piercy's research received the Reading Research Award from the State of Maryland International Reading Association Council. She was honored with the Bailer Award from McDaniel College for her distinguished career in education, and was the recipient of the Court Appointed Special Advocate (CASA) Children's Hero Award. As a teacher, she was named one of five expert teachers by the Maryland State Department of Education.

Thommie's previous publications include her book *Compelling Conversations* (2006), chapters in *Learning and Leading with Habits of Mind* (Costa and Kallick, 2008), *Integrating & Sustaining Habits of Mind* (Costa and Kallick, 2000b), *Activating & Engaging Habits of Mind* (Costa and Kallick, 2000a), *Student Successes with Thinking Maps* (Hyerle, 2004), *Step-Up-To-Excellence* (Duffy, 2002), a contribution to *Reading Essentials* (Routman, 2003), and articles in *The Elementary School Journal* and the *Maryland ASCD Journal.*

In addition to being an author, Thommie is a pre-K–12 reading supervisor in a district outside of Baltimore, Maryland. She is a Professional Development Associate with The Leadership and Learning Center in Englewood, Colorado.

William Piercy, Ph.D., earned his degree in curriculum and instruction with a focus on human resource development from the University of Maryland. He has taught leadership at the graduate level, and provided principal leadership consultation at district and state levels.

Bill and Thommie have co-published a chapter in *Critical Thinking and Reasoning* (Fasko, 2003). They have presented at national conferences, including the ASCD (formerly the Association for Supervision and Curriculum Development), the American Association of School Administrators (AASA), the International Reading Association (IRA), the National Staff Development Council (NSDC), and the International Conference on Critical Thinking.

After working as a high school principal, Bill served as a supervisor in roles including technology, gifted and talented, and business education. Currently, Bill is responsible for professional development, including leadership development, as a supervisor in a district outside of Baltimore, Maryland.

Thommie and Bill share the pleasures of four children, and live with their Saint Bernard on the Shenandoah River adjacent to Harpers Ferry National Historical Park in West Virginia. They enjoy tubing, reading, and long walks with rich conversations. They work in school districts throughout the country in the areas of literacy, leadership, Compelling Conversations, and data-driven decision making. They can be reached at TPiercy@LeadandLearn.com and Piercys@aol.com.

Foreword

By Dr. David Hyerle

Moving Forward into a New Worldview of Literacy

The other day I was sitting comfortably in an easy chair, reading this book in near final form, and looking out the window at a beautiful view of a flowering garden. It was a view nicely cropped by the rectangular wooden window frame. I got up and stepped forward to open the window. Looking out, I realized that no matter how beautiful that view was from my chair, it had been a very limited view. Walking over to the door and then into the garden opened up a new world around me, not limited by what now seemed like the pinhole perception gathered from my chair just moments before. Turning around to look back at the house—at the window and frame—I smiled and recognized again the simple fact that the edges of my peripheral vision forced me to look around if I wanted a more complete view; there will always be multiple perspectives, blind spots in my perception, and endless opportunities for seeing anew.

This book allows us to step forward into a new wider and deeper view of emerging literacy that engages readers in a 360-degree analysis of the field. The carefully crafted insights by Thommie and Bill guide us from our existing "easy chair" perceptions of literacy out into a dynamic garden of multiple literacies in a new age. They help us reframe our view. The authors lead us out into the world for a fresh look around, with an eye toward what *students* are experiencing right now. We are asked to question our fundamental perceptions of literacy without having to leave everything we know behind. Importantly, we are also offered answers, and these are grounded in how we think and reflect, not just how we comprehend.

Educators' present views of literacy do not need to be discarded, but they need to be radically reframed. We step forward too cautiously when bold steps are required. Reading comprehension and critical reading in the disciplines, in the traditional sense, are as important as ever. But through what frame of mind? In past decades, our sights have been set on reading comprehension scores and the manufactured importance of incremental gains in the micro-skills needed to read a page, to the detriment of the big picture. We also need a critical analysis of the different types of texts we read and outward communication using the texting and dynamic graphic tools now available. We have witnessed the birth of new technologies that will change the lives of our childrens' children. We have new forms of all-in-one technologies with video enhancement that are used in almost every walk of life. We may soon have the option of getting Frankensteinian wireless micro computer-pods embedded in our brains—giving a whole new meaning to the idea of "downloading" information (Kurzweil, 2005).

Does some of this look scary? Yes. Yet, I think the only thing that really is scary about the future is that we are not preparing our children for it. As data collectors, kids record and send real-time video clips into the ether, seemingly not caring what they are or where they are going. As Thommie and Bill convey, our youth are *thinking* like freelance reporters on the street—*on their own,* without guidance. Students are doing their own preparation on their handhelds in the back of the room; as we skill, drill, and diminish their capacity to think, they mechanically mark the test prep bubble sheets, slyly texting all the while.

Remembering that a multiple-choice question offers no choice at all—only one right answer—the authors of this book call for a rise to action on the pages ahead. Even though schools have intensely focused on micro-testing of reading skills and linked the results to data-based decisions, the scores have been pretty much level for *decades.* Just take a look at the international PISA (Program for International Student Assessment) results comparing the comprehension scores of students in countries around the world, and you will see the need we have for reframing literacy. By and large, our students are able to "comprehend" at basic levels, but are well below par in their abilities to *think through* complex texts and solve problems using what they read. Of course, the call for a focus on 21st-century skills is on target, but only if we take into account the fact that the performance results remain dramatically off-track for African-American and Hispanic children, and those children in every town in America who live in poverty. It will take more than an emphasis on "academic vocabulary" or another rally 'round about the need for "higher standards" to move this mountain.

It is a difficult task, but this book has joined what we know about literacy development with the depth of thinking that has grown within each discipline. Thommie, Bill, and Brian don't discard what we know, but they show us how to know it differently. They demonstrate that we cannot just sprinkle reading comprehension strategies on top of deep disciplinary content, concepts, and well-honed processes like so much fairy dust on a rich landscape. Students must be able to independently and collaboratively *think* like scientists, *think* like mathematicians, *think* like historians in order to be able to gather, generate, process, and reflect on information as *knowledge.*

Students must be able to take in the disconnected data points streamed from around the world—now often "recorded" by unknowable sources—and connect the dots. They must put this information within the context of what they learn on their own corner of the block, their neighborhood, town, and city, all the while empathizing with and learning from other corners of the world. With this, ultimately, students must be able to think across disciplines, because any problem that they have as individuals or that they inherit from us as a society must be addressed through multiple ways of thinking.

I celebrate this book. The authors, Thommie and Bill Piercy, and contributors Brian Wienholt and Brenda Conley gently challenge us to think about our own perceptions. They don't just critique the existing system of education and paint idealized pictures; they offer well-researched classroom practices, and they also engage us with meaningful practices without falling prey to simplistic and catchy "how-to" and "best practices" solutions. With grace, deep knowledge, and humble questioning, *Disciplinary Literacy: Redefining Deep Understanding and Leadership for 21st-Century Demands* has found the middle path, blending philosophical shifts in pedagogy with clear stepping stones for moving forward into a new worldview of the garden we call literacy.

Foreword

By Dr. Douglas B. Reeves

Putting 21st-Century Literacy within Reach

If we know that literacy is the key to success in every discipline in every school, every year throughout our children's education, then why is it that we traditionally devote fewer hours to literacy with each succeeding year of education? Although chronic low performance in literacy bedevils students and teachers in middle and high school grades, it is a rare 13-year-old student who receives as much deliberate literacy instruction as most second-grade students. The typical excuse for this self-inflicted educational wound is that teachers do not have the time, given the demands of their various subject-matter disciplines, to also address student needs in literacy. Fortunately, Thommie and Bill Piercy offer a practical way out of this dilemma.

Teachers and school administrators will find the following pages immensely useful for three reasons. First, the authors do not compromise on the need for mastery of academic disciplines, such as mathematics, science, and social studies. Their approach to literacy connections is not a diversion away from those subjects, but rather a deeper exploration of each one. They reject explicitly the reasoning that, "We can't devote extra attention to literacy because we must cover the science standards" and "We can't study science until we have mastered literacy." In the chaotic and imperfect world we call school, there are always going to be more demands on the time available to teachers than can be addressed. Therefore, this book is not about what could theoretically be accomplished if all conditions were right. Rather, this book is about how to teach with maximum effectiveness when, inevitably, conditions are *not* right. In our world, students are preoccupied with family and social concerns and affected by learning disabilities, teachers have more content than they can cover and more assessments than they can prepare for, and administrators must consider external and internal demands that seem to increase almost daily. But literacy strategies are not a "zero-sum" game in which a decision to pursue one strategy necessarily means the abandonment of another. Rather, with vivid examples and compelling logic, the authors show how teachers can use literacy to enhance, not reduce, their commitment to disciplinary learning.

Second, this book is full of practical examples, and particularly helpful to social studies teachers, whose curricula have been among the most overloaded in recent decades. While media accounts of social studies standards have been preoccupied with the politically laden decisions surrounding what is included and excluded from state standards, the real scandal is the pervasive expectations that teachers and students can magically absorb and master greater quantities of information in the same quantity of time as in the past. Thommie and Bill Piercy's counsel that we must read and think like historians is helpful not only for students, but for all of us.

Third, this book does an admirable job of demystifying "21st-century skills," a term often distinguished more by the profligate way in which it is inserted into educational conversations than by its practical use in schools. The often-heard mantra that students should "create, communicate, and think critically" in the 21st century, as if they did not need those skills in decades past, has made more than a few people cynical about 21st-century skills. This book, wonderfully free of jargon, addresses the practical issues of how teachers can help students engage in creativity, communication, and critical thinking, while remaining true to the rigors of their academic disciplines.

Teachers, administrators, and university faculty who prepare them could profitably spend time dissecting this book and then committing themselves to the creation of rich and engaging activities for students. Students, too, should join the challenge, becoming co-creators of a new generation of lessons, activities, and assessments. This will be a book that will not be a passing fad, but rather will be an enduring asset to the library of every educator and leader.

Preface

By Dr. Thomasina Piercy

Gearing Up Literacy

Believing new cars with automatic transmissions were a waste of money, my grandfather taught me to drive a vehicle with a stick shift. "Easy on the clutch," or "Release the clutch slowly so the gears can engage," he would say as we rambled along, nearly stalling. Honestly, I had no idea what he was talking about, because there was no map to provide visual understanding of how the different moving parts of the vehicle were intended to work together. Only since we began discussing how the components of disciplinary literacy instruction are analogous to moving gears have I acquired a deeper appreciation for those distant conversations.

Literacy, like the engine, is increasing in complexity. Just as the field of quantum physics now includes groups of "quantum gears" that serve as models for different systems, the field of literacy can benefit from a simple model capable of depicting its complexity, change, and motion. The gear analogy readily depicts literacy's moving parts as paths of action to provide clarity for each concept throughout this book. The Disciplinary Literacy instructional model described within this book respects the unique, rigorous comprehension demands of each content area through guiding deeper understanding. As the gear analogy depicts, each discipline is a vital, independent field of study; however, the motion of 21st-century literacy requires connections between different content areas. Providing instructional direction that honors each content area, while engaging adolescents' critical thinking, results in a depth of understanding.

As technology is catapulting adolescents towards the 22nd century, it is imperative for educators to embrace the potential literacy holds. This book honors today's depth of literacy while "gearing up" instruction with a research-based Disciplinary Literacy model.

As my grandfather would say, "Now's the time to give it some gas!"

Acknowledgments

With strong voices sending clear currents of expectation into the education industry for the 21st and 22nd centuries, it is with much humility that we offer this volume as a contribution to the field of literacy. Our sincere appreciation goes to all those whose voices have enriched our thoughts and guided our writing journey.

Brian Wienholt, M.S., first and foremost, is the teacher every parent would wish his or her child to have the opportunity to learn with. Brian's thoughts, insights, and reflections contributed to our thinking as a Supervisor of Reading and Language Arts for Middle School. Brian is recognized for his teaching, mentoring, and leadership. He is respected for his development of creative opportunities for those with whom he supervises. In addition to authoring a chapter of this book, he co-authored an article for the journal of the Maryland chapter of the ASCD (Association for Supervision and Curriculum Development). As a friend and colleague, Brian has provided many stimulating learning conversations. With his degree in English and passion for reading, Brian's inspiration touches the lives of teachers, students, and all educators.

Todd Chicchirichi, M.S., is a Senior Professional Development and Technology Specialist in Charles Town, West Virginia. Todd specializes in the creation, infusion, and implementation of 21st-century electronic media in the system, school, classroom, and community. Todd is a gifted science educator and a professional staff developer with national, state, regional, and local experience in the areas of instructional technology, curriculum development, and 21st-century learning skills. Todd was the Director of Professional, Leadership, and Technology Development at Regional Educational Service Agency 8 in West Virginia. He is the recipient of several regional, state, and national awards in the area of technology and professional development. Todd's insight, patience, and creative perspective contributed significantly to our final products.

Brenda Conley, Ed.D., a previous Assistant Superintendent of Baltimore City Public Schools Professional and Leadership Development Division, currently specializes in transformational school change and aspiring leadership practices with Towson State University School of Graduate Education. Additionally, Brenda works with the Amprey and Associates Consulting Firm, providing professional and leadership development to school systems across the country. She is a contributing partner with the Towson State University Leadership, Learning, and Professional Development Group. As Brenda continues to work with school systems, schools, and classroom teachers across the country, she is never without a glint in her eye and a wonderful experience to share with one and all. Brenda is a friend of twenty years and one of the most voracious learners we know.

Katie Schellhorn, M.Ed., is the Publishing Manager at The Leadership and Learning Center in Englewood, Colorado. In her role, she not only coordinates and manages all publications; she also devotes significant time to guiding authors. Katie has encouraged us to reach for the stars while keeping us grounded in the realities of publishing. Her reflective ear was always available and her insightful feedback contributed significantly to our final publication. Katie's ability to identify the challenges and barriers we encountered as authors guided our ideas into coherent products. Her degrees in English and curriculum and instruction, and her experience in editing and publishing provide her with a wealth of knowledge and experience that shaped our writing. Katie's strong vision, in addition to her guidance and encouragement, illuminated our path to completion.

We are eternally grateful to the following individuals for their input, enthusiasm, ideas, and support:

Dr. Douglas B. Reeves' support, and that of the remarkable team at The Leadership and Learning Center, have informed our progress. From Dr. David Hyerle's spirited conversations that penetrated our thinking, to Regie Routman's heartfelt letters of love for family and friends, we have been blessed. As a steadfast friend whose warmth penetrates distance, Dr. Art Costa's passion has brought meaning to our efforts daily. Through the years, Jay McTighe's friendship has expanded our understanding about the power of a literacy vision. Dr. Barb Kapinus' critical deep understanding of unfolding policies has blended with her insight about the Common Core State Standards, resulting in rich conversations and direction. Superintendent Barbara Whitecotton's perceptiveness has penetrated the heart of leadership as she has led her district to astounding improvement, while Diane Tusang's insightful special education leadership has contributed vastly to students' literacy improvement. Their insights have significantly informed our thinking.

When considering leaders who have contributed to literacy, no leaders have had more influence than teacher leaders. Lori Thomas, a passionate teacher of literacy, makes a difference in the classroom daily. Teachers such as Lori define dedication at its core. As a high school teacher, Lori inspires a desire to learn within students as they incorporate astounding thinking while overcoming personal limitations. Stephanie Simmons' special education students have achieved significant progress due to her remarkable passion, beliefs, and willingness to communicate with others. Literacy for numerous disciplines resounds within the field of music as Rachel Morgan demonstrates for her students and communicates so eloquently.

Our lives' greatest blessing has been our family, including our children Tracy, Ian, Jody, and Michael, and their gifts of love, laughter, and encouragement for one another and our entire family. We are deeply grateful for having spent much of our professional lives in the excellent school system of Carroll County Public Schools, Maryland, under the recent compassionate, insightful leadership of Superintendent Dr. Charles Ecker.

INTRODUCTION

How Can Disciplinary Literacy Establish Deeper Connections?

By Drs. Thomasina and William Piercy

Connections are all around us. Let's take a look at three specific connections that are the bedrock of literacy for the 21st and 22nd centuries. Enlightening an international audience, Malcolm Gladwell stated, "Mastery cannot be telescoped" (2009b). He explained that the *struggle* is where learning resides. Confirming this thinking, Howard Gardner states that acquiring a disciplined mind is vital, because learners "must see information not as an end in itself" (2008, p. 30). Learners "must be able to think in ways that characterize the major disciplines ... Science, Mathematics, and History and at least one art form" (p. 31). He concludes, "Knowledge of facts is a useful ornament but a fundamentally different undertaking than thinking in a discipline" (p. 32). Having a disciplined mind is the foundation for Disciplinary Literacy.

Disciplinary Literacy research and related literature are disclosing significant findings that dispute long-accepted "reading in the content areas" strategies (McKeown, Beck, and Blake, 2009; Shanahan and Shanahan, 2008; Snow and Moje, 2010; Wineburg, 2007 and 2001). Literacy skills and strategies are not as easily generalized as once thought.

In 1999, Vacca and Vacca said that Content Literacy requires teachers to "show students how to use the reading and writing strategies needed to construct content knowledge" (p. 25). The list of recommended comprehension strategies included reciprocal teaching, question-answer relationships, and think-alouds (p. 53). In many schools, these strategies were integrated in elementary and secondary levels, during both the primary "learning to read years," and later during the intermediate "reading to learn" years. Yes, that's right—every grade, every discipline. The problem was, after the intermediate grades, comprehension instruction stopped. And although the strategies *could* be applied in every discipline, just as we all *could* wear the same one-size-fits-all T-shirt, the strategies didn't fit every discipline any better than that

T-shirt would fit every person. Different disciplines require specific aligned actions for the unique learning that each discipline demands, as practiced by historians, mathematicians, literary critics, and scientists. As the Disciplinary Literacy Tree on the cover and in the Conclusions depict, each discipline's unique expectations of the reader requires instruction aligned with its specific demands. While providing instruction honoring the individual thinking required in each discipline, as represented by different blossoms among the leaves, all contents share an equal need for literacy. It is literacy's strength as a powerful uniting factor that allows each discipline to thrive.

When students incorporate literacy actions with discipline-specific inquiry models, teachers are able to identify students' needs and determine instructional modifications. Explicit instruction of literacy actions results in adolescents being able to transfer these actions when needed as they resurface in different mediums and personal situations.

Providing interactions with the Literacy Action Frameworks (pages 26–59) increases connections between the disciplines of English language arts, history/social studies, science, math, and music. To paraphrase the words of U2 singer and lyricist Bono, these actions make us "one—but not the same," by integrating deep processes and constructed understandings that do not generalize or minimize concepts to serve the pretense of connections, but honor the differences of each discipline. Literacy actions enable adolescents to make sense of the enormous amount of constantly available, changing information. The Disciplinary Literacy inquiry models presented incorporate literacy actions, scaffold comprehension that honors each discipline not only for the purpose of learning specific content, but for the larger outcome of expanding deep understanding that is applicable to different disciplines and life in general.

Disciplined Practice applies leadership constructs which permit leaders to personally own and demonstrate the use of literacy actions to guide teachers and students, rather than outsourcing literacy to professional developers. By personally embracing the literacy actions described throughout this book, leaders can impact every grade, discipline, teacher, and student. The literacy leader's disciplined decision to *regularly* ask targeted questions about every student results in generative Compelling Conversations that improve student progress (Piercy, 2006, p. 34). Disciplined Practice enhances the leader's ability to assess and evaluate student and teacher progress. Is this too much to expect? Perhaps it was in the 20th century. Today, evaluating student progress and determining cause data is a key leadership role.

Can student expectations be achieved when literacy is disconnected from each content area? No! The report on the subject from the Carnegie Corporation, *Time to Act* (2010, p. 52), explains that beyond the typical overall literacy competencies, close attention is needed for the specific literacy competencies within each content area. The Common Core State Standards Initiative (2010), which developed a set of kindergarten through grade 12 education standards in English language arts and mathematics, incorporates broad competencies, including specific literacy actions that are at the heart of curricula. According to Shanahan and Shanahan, "we have spent a century of education beholden to the generalist notion of literacy learning— the idea that if we just provide adequate basic skills, from that point forward kids with adequate background knowledge will be able to read anything successfully" (2008, p. 40). The limited success of the "reading in the content areas" approach is due in part to not recognizing the different comprehension demands of each discipline. For example, reading history as a historian requires deeper analysis and personal investment in understanding the text than applying "reading in the content areas" strategies affords.

Inherent in Disciplinary Literacy is the increasing expectation for students to incorporate research into their reading and writing as depicted in the Common Core State Standards. Backward mapped from the College and Career Readiness Standards to Elementary Standards, a "Research to Build Knowledge" strand for communicating through writing is included for monitoring student progression from elementary grades through college. It is important to note the increased expectations in the Common Core State Standards for students to use technology to gather information through print and digital sources, while incorporating specific literacy actions such as evaluating and analyzing. As a result of students both desiring and being expected to access digital media, the phenomenon of adolescents independently acquiring "citizen journalist" skills is emerging. When students are guided to think and communicate like citizen journalists by questioning the context, questioning unfiltered information, and questioning their own communication, including distribution of information, Art Costa's Habits of Mind (Costa and Kallick, 2008, pp. 18–37) are at work. Our vision for this book is to provide clarity and a fresh, *live* perspective of literacy to provide systemic improvement for literacy achievement.

Vision: Literacy Connections for Adolescents

Learners and leaders will be able to apply dynamic literacy actions and Habits of Mind using the Disciplinary Literacy inquiry model to increase their capacity as critical thinkers, readers, and communicators of multimedia information during their evolving lives.

From Gardner's Disciplined Mind (2008) to current research literature on Disciplinary Literacy, the time has come to provide literacy instruction and leadership that is not outsourced but interconnected throughout district, school, and team leadership. The following chapters bring leaders and learners together by acknowledging the natural connectedness of adolescent literacy.

CHAPTER 1

What Are the Connections between Citizen Journalists and Adolescent Learners?

Why is literacy receiving attention unequaled to other 21st-century skills? From literacy's vibrant beginning on cave walls 30,000 years ago, the pace of change throughout our newly flattened world has induced connectedness. Known as "reading in the content areas," adolescent literacy strategies were based on a narrow concept of literacy for 40 years. The newer term, Disciplinary Literacy, is characterized by a focus on deeper understanding, dynamic connections with information, and technological advances, including a recognition that the Internet is not just an electronic screen, but an extension of our adolescents' lives.

Decisions regarding learning and leadership have demonstrated a need for Disciplined Practice that incorporates literacy actions. Literacy actions inform our decisions as leaders, teachers, and learners.

Remember how our grandparents' coffee actually percolated? The beverage's strength was judged by seeing the richness of color through the glass dome and listening to the bubbling. The brew engaged us before the first taste. Not a simple process, brewing coffee required specific actions and content knowledge beyond adding scoops of coffee to a filtered basket, pushing a button, and waiting.

Yesteryear's coffee was not easy to make, but it engaged the coffee drinker in the process, creating a richer, more enduring experience than can be enjoyed from the taste alone. When literacy outcomes include the use of literacy actions such as evaluating and Habits of Mind, enduring learning crosses over into students' outside of school lives, as described in the Common Core State Standards (2010), which stipulate that expectations for critical thinking must transfer beyond achievement of isolated skills. Specifically, these standards "lay out a vision of what it means to be a literate person in the 21st century" (p. 3). Not only as students, teachers, and leaders, but as citizens, we have a responsibility and a duty to understand and apply literacy—not outsource it. Our students need to believe they will use what they know in their changing lives and exciting futures. As the literacy action stories in this chapter indicate, together we can better understand the world and guide students to value their own positive presence.

> *Literacy has been education's quiet soldier, neatly organized within the content areas of English language arts and reading.*

Literacy has been education's quiet soldier, neatly organized within the content areas of English language arts and reading, guarding for Americans the adherence to standard written English. No longer constrained, literacy is evolving in significance and complexity.

An example of the degree of complexity currently impacting literacy is the tumultuous decline of newspaper readership. Publishers are posing questions similar to those being asked in education as a result of the impact the economic crisis is having on local school districts. How can our nation's leading, yet financially destitute, newspapers, such as the *New York Times* and the *Washington Post,* trapped in an unhealthy economy, make wrenching decisions that will have successful outcomes? Likewise, how can educators who are experiencing devastating economic challenges navigate unknown terrain toward uncertain student outcomes? Perhaps the larger problem is that the student outcomes that were desired in the past no longer align with today's needs. Can accurate decisions about instruction and leadership be made when the goals we are striving for are not closely aligned with students' future needs? "Buckle up," advises a *Washington Post* column (Alexander, 2009) about the changes it would make to address decreasing revenues. Yes, education, newspapers, and literacy-related businesses are experiencing significant transformations.

When dealing with tumultuous change, the science of Chaos Theory (see Exhibit 1.1), specifically the phenomenon known as the "butterfly effect," can enlighten understanding about how small changes, such as Disciplinary Literacy instruction and Disciplined Practice leadership, can result in significant outcomes, such as literacy connections (see Exhibit 1.2).

Just as Gardner explained, "Respectful and ethical minds cannot be outsourced" (2008, p. 7); leaders can no longer outsource literacy to others without assuming accountability themselves.

When system and school leaders breathe literacy into every decision, they model Disciplined Practice leadership described in Chapter 3, and facilitate opportunities for iterations to flow throughout the community. It is the continuous presence of clear, informed literacy behaviors and expectations within schools that can eventually shape current chaotic literacy conditions. Together, we teachers, leaders, business people, and citizens are at the border of an unknown 21st–22nd century terrain where opportunities exist for maximum literacy exchanges and creativity. It is here

EXHIBIT 1.1 **Chaos Theory and Literacy Connections**

Although the word "chaos" implies disorder and confusion, **Chaos Theory** is about finding underlying order in randomness. Chaos Theory guides understanding by establishing order during times of confusion. It is with careful consideration that we refer to Chaos Theory in this chapter about literacy. The science behind the theory is complex, and the connections presented in this chapter are not intended to simplify concepts. Rather, we are applying learnings derived from our study of this theory to better understand relationships between expected 21st-century literacy outcomes and existing educational conditions (Piercy and Piercy, 2003, p. 189).

Can leaders apply principles of Chaos Theory to assist with the understanding of literacy as it is exploding into the scene of education? To begin with, Chaos Theory dissolves barriers such as those that have separated disciplines into disconnected subjects. This specific characteristic of removing barriers spiked our interest in Chaos Theory, since literacy *is* the connecting link between each discipline. Exhibit 1.2 defines attributes of Chaos Theory (Set A) and its connections with literacy (Set B). It is the *intersection* of the attributes of these two sets, as depicted in the Set B examples, that explains the significance of the connections between the abstract scientific theory and the concrete direction for literacy provided in these chapters. It is helpful for leaders to recognize the cause-effect impact of Chaos Theory on instruction and learning. For example, when leaders are intentional about applying specific literacy actions by incorporating aligned reflective questions, fractals of literacy iterate naturally into instruction, student learning, and life decisions.

that we can determine literacy outcomes that are not only *desired* but also *aligned* with adolescents' future needs.

Global changes and the resulting flattening world of education (Darling-Hammond, 2010) are contributing to the need for new desired outcomes for adolescent literacy. One transformational change impacting the desired outcomes is the decline in readership of traditional newspapers. This is not having just a "butterfly" effect; it's more like the flapping of a pterodactyl's wings! One immediate outcome is the decrease in the number of reporters within the White House pressroom. Today, our president can and does communicate with millions of citizens directly using a multitude of technologies that were not available to the founding fathers. Imagine citizens' questions about ethics when Thomas Jefferson became the first president to

EXHIBIT 1.2   **Chaos Theory and Literacy Connections**

Set A CHAOS THEORY	Set B LITERACY
The Butterfly Effect: Very small changes in initial conditions result in wide, unexpected outcomes. Therefore, early decisions are vital to results.	**The Butterfly Effect:** Initial central office conversations about literacy establish conditions that will impact future decisions. **Example of Literacy Connection:** The decision to establish a literacy vision, a mission, and goals increases student expectations, changes question types, and initiates dialogue across disciplines by increasing opportunities for literacy connections.
Fractal: A single repetition of detail but in a smaller, descending scale.	**Fractal:** A data-based decision made by the central office is repeated in each school's decisions. **Example of Literacy Connection:** The decision to develop district-level formative assessments in different disciplines and monitor progress is replicated when each school develops Common Formative Assessments (Ainsworth and Viegut, 2006) and frequently monitors their students' literacy progress. Following the Data Team meetings (Besser, Almeida, Anderson-Davis, Flach, Kamm, and White, 2008), administrators take SMART goals along during walk-throughs to monitor the process of aligning of instruction with goals.
Iteration: The process through which multiple fractals, or details, are created that takes the same steps to a smaller scale.	**Iteration:** A leader, a teacher, and then a student display specific "literacy actions." A literacy action is incorporated into the leadership process by the school leader while monitoring student progress, then is included in instruction by teachers, and applied by students for learning in different disciplines and in their lives. **Example of Literacy Connection:** A principal incorporates the literacy leadership action of "inferencing" during a conversation about students' progress with a teacher. The teacher repeats the use of inferencing when talking to individual students about progress. Students apply inferencing to monitor their assignments and improve their progress before the end of the semester. They also apply inferencing to improve their deeper comprehension of primary documents in history.
Continuous Pressure: A process that shapes chaotic behaviors.	**Continuous Pressure:** Processes such as providing Disciplined Practice leadership, Compelling Conversations, walk-throughs, and instructional rounds. **Example of Literacy Connection:** After holding Compelling Conversations, the administrator takes the information and decisions gained from those conversations along on walk-throughs to support literacy alignment in instruction and student learning.

use mass communication to his advantage through the *National Intelligencer* newspaper in the year 1800. Two hundred years later, we continue to see the dust settle. Now, immediate raw data is available to everyone—*unfiltered by reporters' critical questions.* As a result, students are becoming "adolescent citizen journalists." There is an increasing need for adolescents to depend on their own devices, comprised of a combination of literacy actions. Literacy actions are specific skills, strategies, and types of thinking. They facilitate deeper levels of understanding, which adolescents are able to transfer into their lives. Literacy actions are intentional actions used to increase meaning. They are fully described in the Literacy Action Frameworks beginning on page 26. Habits of Mind (Costa and Kallick, 2008), presented in Chapter 4, delve for underlying truth and guide accurate decisions.

HOW ARE ADOLESCENT CITIZEN JOURNALISTS CHANGING INSTRUCTION?

As a result of vast shifts in economics and technology, the phenomenon of the citizen journalist has begun to take hold. Thinking and communicating like a citizen journalist is the ability to communicate the daily events of one's life, from the *context* in which they are happening, to the world in which people live and work. Citizen journalists do not have professional training as journalists. They use technology to immediately communicate with global audiences when responding to and reporting news and information. As citizen journalists, adolescents are at the right place at the right time to capture events as they unfold on personal electronic communication devices. They report unfolding events through their *personal perspective.*

Following the 2010 State of the Union Address, President Obama granted the first live interview from the White House to YouTube, in a forum referred to as "CitizenTube." *This was prior to interviews by any reporters from the press core or networks.* Every question came directly from citizens, unscreened. With more than 11,000 questions submitted, it is clear that the concept of the "citizen journalist" is a 21st-century phenomenon that is quickly evolving, apparently from a long thirst. As "direct-to-you" communication expands in our culture, including communication from the president of the United States, citizens young and old need to critically evaluate information, even information from reliable resources. Take the whitehouse.gov free app (application) that provides immediate access to citizens via their iPhones as an example: the moment statements are released from the office of the president, they are directly transmitted to the people, unfiltered and unquestioned. Such immediate access to news has transformed television's bedrock evening news programs into "old news" programs. They are less enticing, with fewer "breaking news" banners, due to the fact that significant events were transmitted the

As a result of emerging citizen journalist behaviors, adolescents need to develop critical literacy expertise at a previously unforeseen level.

moment they happened. Having immediate access to enormous amounts of sensitive information at every level requires a depth of literacy, which is represented in the Literacy Action Frameworks. As a result of emerging citizen journalist behaviors, adolescents need to develop critical literacy expertise at a previously unforeseen level.

What desired outcomes would align with the future of adolescents? Successful outcomes would need to increase *all* students' expertise and ethics; they would need to be capable of effectively incorporating literacy real-time, to adapt to the swirling changes of the present *while* predicting appropriate adjustments for future changes. Does this seem alarming?

Fear can befriend change when it is not understood.

Since fear can befriend change when it is not understood, to better understand recent changes in literacy, let's take a look at the *pace* of change, and its dire implications, illustrated by the recent news items listed in Exhibit 1.3.

These separate news items over time established a *bits and pieces* linear organization pattern—and that's all. Each of these separate news stories

 EXHIBIT 1.3 **News Items**

News Items
- Presidential voter outreach campaign
- California bailout
- Junk bonds are the culprit
- U.S. treasury rescue
- Ponzi investment fraud
- Goldman Sachs bankrupt
- Wall Street vs. Main Street
- Panic about foreclosure
- AIG bailout by taxpayers
- Merrill Lynch bankrupt
- Plummeting global economy
- Bailing out the car industry
- Three billion apps downloaded
- CitizenTube poses 11,000 questions to president
- Stimulus Bill—$787 billion

was significant, yet when each story is *connected* to the others, profound ramifications can become clear.

As exemplified in the news stories mentioned in Exhibit 1.3, determining connections between linear details is a focus of the important, timely Carnegie Corporation comprehensive research on adolescent literacy (2010, pp. 13–19 and 79) in addition to research and literature from experts in the field (Shanahan and Shanahan, 2008; Shanahan, 2009; Snow and Moje, 2010; Wineburg, 2007 and 2001) who have defined the

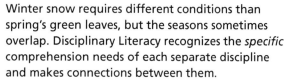

There is a need for new, discipline-specific instruction to scaffold adolescents' understanding as they build connections within a text.

need for *new, discipline-specific instruction* to scaffold adolescents' understanding as they build connections within a text by *analyzing* the context, text, and subtexts. The emerging Disciplinary Literacy constructs are designed on the premise that as text complexity increases, each discipline requires unique strategies beyond those offered by general "reading in the content areas" strategies to fully comprehend meaning.

Winter snow requires different conditions than spring's green leaves, but the seasons sometimes overlap. Disciplinary Literacy recognizes the *specific* comprehension needs of each separate discipline and makes connections between them.

Literacy actions support connections among all disciplines, as spring overlaps with winter in the photo, by recognizing literacy's "phase space," where all possible states of a system can be represented.

How can we prepare students to live in this new world they are inheriting *while* making it better? To begin, it is helpful to understand how the devastating events noted earlier in the news stories changed the current social, political, and media paradigms of our day-to-day existence in unforeseen ways. Yes, *unforeseen*, even though we are living in an age of 24-hour access to enormous amounts of information. What literacy actions, such as *questioning* and *evaluating*, were our most respected, responsible adults, businesses, and banks *not* applying in the situations described in the news stories in Exhibit 1.3? What questions were *not* asked of Bernie Madoff by his thousands of clients as they handed him $50 billion? What *evaluation* skills were *not* applied by mega-firms that could have prevented large corporate bailouts by the federal government? On an individual scale, what literacy actions were financial institutions *not* applying when they provided approval for mortgages of one or more homes to citizens with insufficient incomes? These decisions appear so absurd, one would believe them to be untrue.

Comprehending world changes being rapidly fired into our consciousness requires a capacity to integrate information for meaning, form questions, and develop patterns of understanding. This approach is quite different from the strategies that were used to process the packaged information and isolated facts that were available in the past. Now that they have *unlimited* access to raw data, truth is in the hands of citizen journalists. In February 2010, the *New York Times* reported that for the first time, a George Polk Award, from Long Island University, was bestowed on an anonymous citizen journalist (McFadden, 2010). It was reported that the panel wanted to acknowledge the role of ordinary citizens in the dissemination of images and news in times of tumult and recognize the efforts of the people. To accommodate citizen journalism around the globe for the mobile Internet age, CNN has a free app for submitting news from iPhones (www.cnn.com/mobile/iphone/). The company states the content "is not edited or fact-checked." Adolescents have enormous opportunities to make rapid impact around the globe. What can teachers do to prepare adolescents for the vital role of becoming citizen journalists?

The citizen journalist components in Exhibits 1.4a and 1.4b guide students in *applying* literacy actions and Habits of Mind while incorporating basic publishing standards, such as using "just the facts," avoiding hearsay, omitting irrelevant opinion, giving credit, and identifying sources (Palevsky, 2009). The following questions guide adolescents' thinking as citizen journalists:

1. What questions do I need to ask myself to determine the *context* of the source of information?

2. What questions do I need to ask myself when reading *unfiltered* information?

3. What questions do I need to ask *about* myself before preparing information for distribution?

The specific questions on the citizen journalist filter (Exhibit 1.4a) and student response form (Exhibit 1.4b) create a Path of Action for applying literacy actions and Habits of Mind when reacting to information.

Why was the public caught off-guard during the recent devastating economic downturn? Could it be that members of the general public have been experiencing the news as outsiders? Polished and controlled, the news media have provided a perspective, over which viewers have had little control. Creating a disconnected realm,

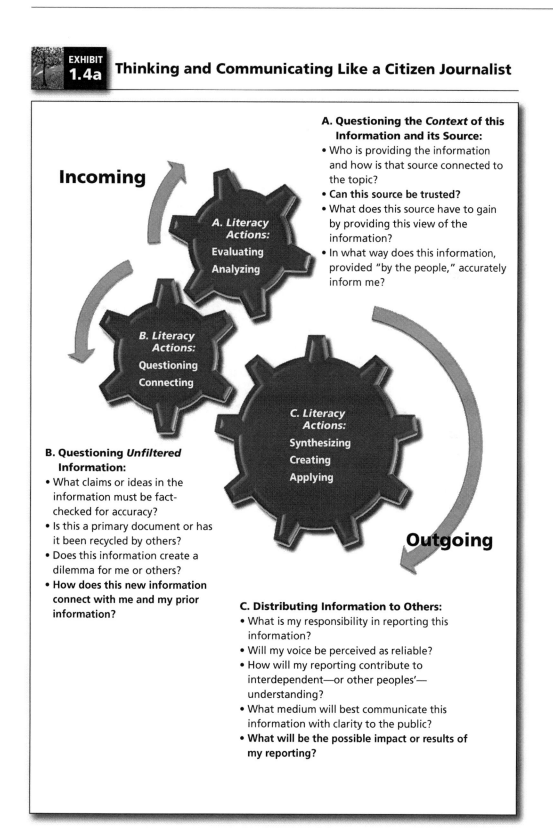

EXHIBIT 1.4a Thinking and Communicating Like a Citizen Journalist

Incoming

A. Literacy Actions:
Evaluating
Analyzing

B. Literacy Actions:
Questioning
Connecting

C. Literacy Actions:
Synthesizing
Creating
Applying

Outgoing

A. Questioning the *Context* of this Information and its Source:
- Who is providing the information and how is that source connected to the topic?
- **Can this source be trusted?**
- What does this source have to gain by providing this view of the information?
- In what way does this information, provided "by the people," accurately inform me?

B. Questioning *Unfiltered* Information:
- What claims or ideas in the information must be fact-checked for accuracy?
- Is this a primary document or has it been recycled by others?
- Does this information create a dilemma for me or others?
- **How does this new information connect with me and my prior information?**

C. Distributing Information to Others:
- What is my responsibility in reporting this information?
- Will my voice be perceived as reliable?
- How will my reporting contribute to interdependent—or other peoples'—understanding?
- What medium will best communicate this information with clarity to the public?
- **What will be the possible impact or results of my reporting?**

EXHIBIT 1.4b **Thinking and Communicating Like a Citizen Journalist Student Response Form**

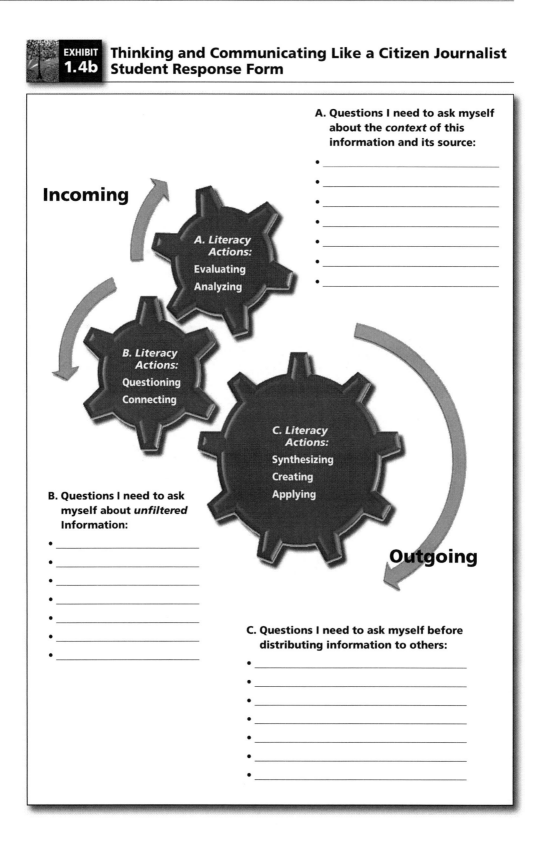

Incoming

A. Literacy Actions:
Evaluating
Analyzing

B. Literacy Actions:
Questioning
Connecting

C. Literacy Actions:
Synthesizing
Creating
Applying

Outgoing

A. Questions I need to ask myself about the *context* of this information and its source:

- _____
- _____
- _____
- _____
- _____
- _____
- _____

B. Questions I need to ask myself about *unfiltered* Information:

- _____
- _____
- _____
- _____
- _____
- _____
- _____

C. Questions I need to ask myself before distributing information to others:

- _____
- _____
- _____
- _____
- _____
- _____
- _____

the "truth" has been communicated based on the perceptions of a few. Constructing a buffer between the actual events (the "primary document" sources for news reports) and the readership, the existence of news reporting absorbed many opportunities that might have been available for citizens to apply the literacy actions, such as *analyzing* and *inferencing*, upon which literacy is crafted. Primary documents and raw data provide adults and adolescents with rich literacy opportunities.

The same holds true for the content of many school textbooks, which are presented as factual accounts. Citizens became dependent upon news reporters' and textbook authors' literacy skills, (and vulnerable to how those reporters and writers chose to apply them), while their own literacy skills remained unchallenged.

How is the fact that the public was caught off-guard by the most severe economic downturn since the Great Depression any different from the way students have been experiencing public education? Avoidance of difficult decisions is placing additional literacy responsibility into the hands of our adolescents. Time had provided an opportunity to improve, but we didn't take it. Truthfully, we can't say *we* had reason to be caught off-guard, as Chuck Todd (2008) explained, because the National Assessment of Educational Progress (NAEP) and other agencies had been making disturbing data available for decades.

> *Avoidance of difficult decisions is placing additional literacy responsibility into the hands of our adolescents.*

It is true that literacy is characterized by continuous change. In essence, literacy itself is *redefining* what it is. Likewise, adolescents are changing literacy. One high school student commented with frustration about how the restriction of Internet use at school forces kids to use their iPods in the bathrooms! Is this what we want for students? How beneficial it would be to create opportunities to guide adolescents in making responsible decisions. Are we educators reaching a point of literacy bewilderment? That depends on your perspective.

When I saw a black bear from inside our house, my view was buffered by our four brick walls.

LITERACY PERSPECTIVES INFORM UNDERSTANDING

What is the relationship between literacy perspective and deep understanding? How important is perspective for acquiring understanding? Imagine how our neighbor felt upon opening her door and coming face-to-face with a black bear standing on its hind legs. Quite a personal perspective!

Yet, when I watched the bear roaming outside from inside the four walls of our home, I calmly grabbed my iPhone to e-mail the exciting picture to our children. Quite a different perspective from that of my neighbor. My view was buffered; I was on the inside, safe, because I didn't have to deal with the "primary document"—the bear—on the same level that our neighbor did. Then one day I ran into the bear while I was walking outside, and suddenly I gained a new appreciation for my neighbor's view of the bear. When they are buffered by four walls, decisions are less demanding of our skills and expertise. Would *you* choose to open the door?

Malcolm Gladwell explained during a presentation at the American Association of School Administrators' 2010 superintendents' conference that educators have worked within the safety of four walls that education has erected around itself. Upon listening to this message, we visualized these walls as the educational research, philosophies, leaders selected from within districts, and specific college degrees that keep the field of education pure from outside influence. However, global changes *outside* the four walls are having a major impact on education and learning (Exhibit 1.5). It is time to consider learning as something that is connected with world events. Global changes are now our houseguests. Let's extend our welcome with enthusiasm.

Did the "caught off-guard" public really want to know that unemployment was artificially low? Did they want to know that the high rates of home ownership were due to risky loans? Or that the fine line between optimistic views and intentional deception in some large financial corporations' reports was exceptionally frail? Safety within the four walls of education has been a 20th-century shield from reality for us all.

> *Now the door to the future of literacy is ajar—pried open by adolescents.*

The literacy challenge *is* in our faces. Standing on its hind legs, it is creating anxiety while growing stronger—daily. Now the door to the future of literacy is ajar—pried open by adolescents.

Never again will students enter school having experienced only the technologies of pencils and books that were literacy's bailiwick for hundreds of years. With every aspect of literacy rapidly changing, from reading to composing and communicating, the idea that the field of education can recede behind four walls to write more five-year plans is a concept belonging to a previous era. Today's distinctly different literacy realm includes the constructs of continuous change *and* rapid communication—each a serious dynamic in its own right—let

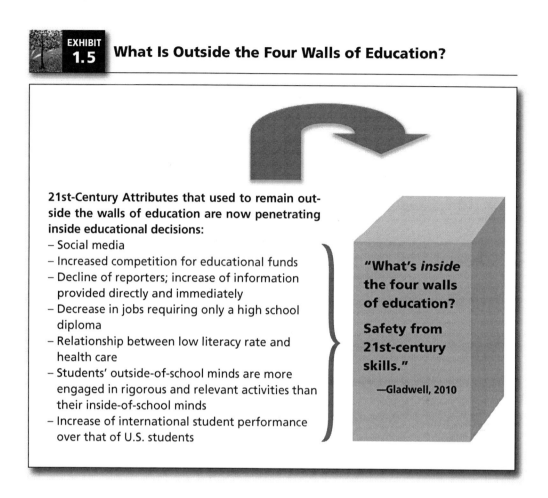

EXHIBIT 1.5   What Is Outside the Four Walls of Education?

21st-Century Attributes that used to remain outside the walls of education are now penetrating inside educational decisions:

- Social media
- Increased competition for educational funds
- Decline of reporters; increase of information provided directly and immediately
- Decrease in jobs requiring only a high school diploma
- Relationship between low literacy rate and health care
- Students' outside-of-school minds are more engaged in rigorous and relevant activities than their inside-of-school minds
- Increase of international student performance over that of U.S. students

"What's *inside* the four walls of education?

Safety from 21st-century skills."

—Gladwell, 2010

alone when experienced together. Timely recommendations are needed to inform today's decisions.

Yes; literacy is an in-your-face bear!

What is it like to look literacy in the face? On a daily basis, fresh literacy terms fly across our screens and desks as fast as new literacy product ads fill our electronic mailboxes. Like politicians facing a vote on a multi-billion-dollar, 1,000-page bill that they may not have had time to read, we must peer into a wall of recent guidelines and make decisions daily, because students cannot wait for us to catch up. They are in our schools today, learning with or without us. Fortunately, national organizations and publications are providing support and direction for these complex literacy problems.

LITERACY RESOURCES: WHAT? WHY? WHO SAYS?

Adolescents, teachers, and leaders must be able to assess raw slices of unfiltered information and *synthesize* it into knowledge that can be readily understood and communicated. The century-long "generalist notion of literacy learning—the idea that if we just provide adequate basic skills, from that point forward kids with background knowledge will be able to read anything successfully . . . has changed" (Shanahan and Shanahan, 2008). As Tim Shanahan explained (2009), the basic skills "vaccination" concept does not hold for content beyond elementary school. Few blue-collar jobs requiring only low levels of literacy exist. Basic reading skills and strategies are not sufficient to expand the mental fluency needed for *applying* information that is increasingly fragmented (Hyerle, 2009, p. 5).

Think about it: in a short time frame, nearly every national educational organization has distributed updated literacy research and documents to guide state and local education agencies. These documents contain dynamic literacies across all disciplines for evolving academic, career, and personal needs, yet honor the unique demands of each. Intriguing reads? Well, yes, but the potential for brain-blur exists for principals and teachers consumed with day-to-day responsibilities to their students. Therefore, for easy access we are including direct connections to information, research, reports, publications, and legislation. The synthesis in Exhibit 1.6 of recent documents and national publications provides a thumbnail view of the drivers of today's adolescent literacy reform, along with contacts for easy access that shaped our thinking for this book (see the References section for full listings).

> Literacy's unpredictability challenges leaders as the fire line of uncertainty intensifies with new national expectations.

The release of just one of the documents listed in Exhibit 1.6 could have set school systems into a tailspin. The nearly concurrent release of these publications is creating an awkward, edgy hesitancy for leaders, who are increasingly searching for a different dynamic for literacy leadership (see Chapter 3). Literacy's unpredictability challenges leaders as the fire line of *uncertainty* intensifies with new national expectations. "Americans have more to fear from the prospect that the instructional-technology revolution will so overwhelm citizens with competing facts and competing opinions that they will give up their freedom in order to gain some degree of *certainty,* than they have to fear from economic competition from around the world" (Schlechty, 2009, p. 16). Combining these documents with ones being released by states and districts to align their curriculum with the recommendations of the Common Core State Standards Initiative (2010) increases complexity and anxiety, as the literacy bear gets closer.

HOW IS LITERACY RESEARCH PROVIDING DIRECTION?

Today, the expanding economy and the needs of a diverse student population overwhelm traditional definitions of literacy that are focused on reading, writing, speaking and lis-

EXHIBIT 1.6   **Literacy Publications, Research, and Resources**

Title of Publication	Author(s)/Website/Publisher
Changing Literacies for Changing Times	Hoffman and Goodman, 2009, Routledge
Common Core State Standards	National Governors Association Center for Best Practices and Council of Chief State School Officers, 2010, www.corestandards.org
Rigorous Curriculum Design	Ainsworth, 2010, Lead + Learn Press
"About the Elementary and Secondary Education Act"	Dennis, 2009, State of Washington, Office of the Superintendent of Public Instruction, www.k12.wa.us/esea/
Five Minds for the Future	Gardner, 2008, Harvard Business School Press
Leading Change in Your School	Reeves, 2009, ASCD
"New Bloom's Taxonomy"	Overbaugh and Schultz, 2009, www.odu.edu/educ/roverbau/Bloom/blooms_taxonomy.htm
Outliers: The Story of Success *What the Dog Saw*	Gladwell, 2008, Little, Brown and Company Gladwell, 2009, Little Brown and Company
Visual Tools for Transforming Information into Knowledge	Hyerle, 2009, Corwin Press
"P-21 Framework Outcomes—Interdisciplinary Themes for Core Subjects"	Partnership for 21st Century Skills, 2009, www.21stcenturyskills.org/
Schooling by Design	Wiggins and McTighe, 2007, ASCD
"Standards for the Assessment of Reading and Writing 21st Century Literacies"	National Council of Teachers of English, 2009, www.ncte.org/standards/assessmentstandards
"Teaching Disciplinary Literacy to Adolescents"	Shanahan and Shanahan, 2008, *Harvard Educational Review*
"The International Society for Technology in Education (ISTE) National Educational Technology Standards and Performance Indicators for Administrators (2009)"	International Society for Technology in Education, 2009, www.iste.org/NETS/ (click on "NETS for Administrators 2009")
Time to Act: An Agenda for Advancing Adolescent Literacy for College and Career Success	Carnegie Corporation. Carnegie Council on Advancing Adolescent Literacy, 2010, www.carnegie.org/literacy, Cavanaugh Press

Notice how pressure tightly compacting snow on these branches transformed it into ice. Similarly, outside societal pressures are shifting the internal structures of "reading in the content area" strategies into Disciplinary Literacy constructs.

tening. A 21st-century understanding of literacy must incorporate all conventional attributes while expanding to include processes capable of manipulating and creating new information. To begin with, society's cultural beliefs about literacy have increased over time, *compacting* the expectations and political pressures for student learning.

Falling one at a time, expectations, like single flakes of snow, can go unnoticed until they accumulate. Packed tightly by external pressures, expectations condense. With pressure over time, internal structures change. In the way that individual snowflakes change into ice sheets, the internal structures of adolescent literacy contained in "reading in the content area" strategies are changing into Disciplinary Literacy constructs. The one-size-fits-all literacy shoe factory is out of business. Our students need us to grab hold of literacy's unique qualities, because our world is being *fueled* by the dynamic, abundant, free energy generated by the fresh turbines of literacy. How can we tap into the dynamic nature of literacy to ignite the unique needs of different disciplines? Where do we begin developing understanding about literacy for today's intermediate and adolescent students? Let's get started by clarifying the multiple skills, strategies, and processes of literacy that have evolved.

To provide clarity, Tim Shanahan, past president of the International Reading Association, contrasted skills with strategies (2009). Typically, reading instruction has emphasized comprehension skills. He defined "skills" as having a single step that is intended to be used quickly and without conscious intention, as in the literal recall of information. On the other hand, "strategies," according to Shanahan, are multistep processes applied intentionally and metacognitively. But the term "skills," as viewed by the Partnership for 21st Century Skills (2009), incorporates creativity, innovation, critical thinking, and problem solving, plus communication and collaboration. These skills, as stated under their rainbow Framework for 21st Century Learning, are substantially different from Shanahan's definition. In addition, David Hyerle (2009, p. xiii) explains that the concept of "process" is "the highest form of learning and the most appropriate base for curriculum change." He says, "It is through process that we can employ knowledge not merely as a composite of information, but as a system for continuous learning." Notice how the definitions of skills are *different* in these works. Yet, their respective definitions for processes and skills contain similarities. Hold on—screaming about discrepancies gets us nowhere. Questioning will help us move forward. Why do the edges of meaning remain fuzzy even when defining such simple terms as skills, strategies, and processes? Remember ... the linear world that we are comfortable with, including its narrow, tested definitions and labels, thrived during the 20th century, when our expectations were different. So where does that leave us today?

Wineburg (2001, p. viii) explains that complex meaning is acquired not through labels, but through *a depth of understanding*. He says that labeling, rather than trying to understand the concepts, leads to discussions of pedagogy. Our quest for understanding literacy must accept complexity, beginning with the fundamental definitions. Should the lack of agreed-upon definitions, as we discussed for skills, strategies, and processes, render us bewildered? No. Accepting complexity means literacy must be grounded in *common understandings*, unlike simple labeling. Therefore, rather than entering into a semantics debate over the correct labeling of specific skills, strategies, or process categories, the literacy components identified in this book are referred to as literacy actions. These actions are presented in depth with Literacy Action Frameworks (pages 26–59). Although we recognize each skill, strategy, and process serves a variety of purposes for the reader, the concept of literacy actions respects complexity by focusing on a *depth of understanding*.

HOW CAN LITERACY ACTIONS GUIDE INSTRUCTION?

To provide clarity, and to put that literacy stake in the ground from which concrete decisions about literacy instruction can be made, this chapter includes a focus on specific actions from a wide variety of traditional and newer literacy skills, strategies, and processes. The term "literacy actions" avoids labeling confusion between skills, strategies, or processes, and provides consistency. Identifying specific actions supports transfer into leadership and into all content areas.

Which literacy actions *must be* taught to provide our students with the capacity for engaging in and understanding the evolving complexities of life?

During morning walks in fresh snow, it is easy to notice how the entire terrain, including paths that existed just hours before, becomes obscured, making it

> *It is only while trudging through a changing, unfamiliar landscape that each step is carefully considered, unlike walking briskly along paths worn with experience.*

When the ground is blanketed in snow, it is impossible to discern the trail from the forest bed; similarly, the plethora of new literacies blanketing education's landscape is resulting in uncertainty about direction.

difficult to discern the trail from the forest bed. The plethora of new literacies blanketing education's traditional landscape is resulting in frustrating uncertainty about next steps. Yet, it is only while trudging through a changing, unfamiliar landscape that each step is carefully considered, unlike walking briskly along paths worn with experience. A snow-drenched terrain increases our analysis of every decision. Perhaps the magnitude of current change and its inherent chaos is just what is needed to nudge educators to analyze literacy practices born in past eras. Literacy objectives based on classical and current taxonomy models, from Bloom (1956) to Marzano and Kendall (2007), have been vital in aligning curricula, but have they sufficiently integrated literacy into the neural pathways of adolescent thinking? What researched adjustments based upon the needs of today's citizenry will literacy actions be asked to address?

Shanahan responds to teacher frustration about the fact that current researchers are decrying over-reliance on the teaching of comprehension strategies, yet those very strategies are included in most reading series and curriculum documents. "You want to get it right, but it is so hard with so many different experts and so many different opinions. What is the right answer?" (2009). Shanahan explains that instruction has been all about the reading strategies and not the text. How true! Walking through classrooms with walls covered with posters of strategy checklists such as "FATP-P" and "Stop-Ask-Fix" makes it difficult to not be distracted. Researchers McKeown, Beck, and Blake (2009) and Shanahan (2009) are recommending that strategy teaching be minimized. Snow and Moje concur: "Making readers aware of skills they automatically employ or strategies they don't need may actually interfere with comprehension" (2010, p. 67). Yes, this is a shift from decades focused mainly upon strategy instruction. They explain that adolescents need to be *engaged*. Hattie concurs: "Curriculum guidance should draw from the central concepts and modes of inquiry in that discipline, and it should itself be disciplined, creating a lean and thoughtful schema of the knowledge base in a domain in ways that allow important ideas and understanding to be constructed, not an overwhelming laundry list of facts. It should ... incorporate the important modes of inquiry in that domain ... enabling knowledge not just to be recalled but to be applied in ways that *analyze, integrate,* and use *understanding* in transferable ways" (2009, p. 297). The literacy actions identified in Exhibit 1.7 include those proven successful in taxonomies and additional research-based components. They facilitate increased understanding that adolescents are able to transfer into their lives.

EXHIBIT 1.7   **Literacy Actions for the 21st and 22nd Centuries**

Literacy Actions: Literacy actions are specific, intentional actions used to increase understanding.	Sets of Literacy Actions: Combining literacy actions increases deeper understanding.
Analyzing	Analyzing, Evaluating, Inferring, Connecting
Applying	Applying, Connecting, Synthesizing, Understanding
Creating	Creating, Problem Solving, Exploring, Questioning, Communicating
Evaluating	Evaluating, Predicting, Judging, Reasoning, Legitimizing
Exploring	Exploring, Sharing, Accessing, Applying, Questioning, Inferring, Connecting, Remembering, Creating
Inferring	Inferring, Reasoning, Analyzing, Connecting, Creating, Filtering/Cycling
Judging	Judging, Evaluating, Analyzing, Arguing
Monitoring	Monitoring, Analyzing, Evaluating, Synthesizing, Questioning, Filtering/Cycling
Questioning	Questioning, Filtering/Cycling, Evaluating, Creating, Summarizing, Analyzing, Synthesizing
Synthesizing	Synthesizing, Connecting, Questioning, Filtering/Cycling, Reasoning, Creating
Understanding	Understanding, Remembering, Monitoring, Accessing, Using Prior Knowledge, Connecting, Synthesizing

The literacy actions are continuously evolving, and are incorporated within the alignment of learning, leadership, and life connections as evidenced in this chapter. These actions appeared frequently throughout recently published national frameworks and the Common Core State Standards Initiative recommendations. It is the application of literacy actions in the context of life that permits understanding to seep into learners' pores.

Continuous change is challenging, but it does not need to be a paralyzing aspect of educational progress. Recently, a curriculum director from the Midwest explained, "We are not planning to develop formative assessments just yet. We do not want to get into the curriculum. It's too overwhelming. So, we are just focusing on instruction." Did you hear the weight of uncertainty become an anchor preventing progress? Although instruction may appear to be an easier goal, without aligned curriculum and assessments, instruction cannot be guaranteed or viable (Marzano, 2003, p. 24). Continuing to make decisions underneath the radar of literacy's demands to avoid intense conversations and potential resistance can result in students having *unguaranteed* skills for 21st-century demands. The following questions offer direction for literacy:

1. What core literacy actions are vital to prepare students for 21st-century productive lives?

2. To increase literacy throughout students' lives, how can literacy actions be taught for understanding?

The core literacy actions described in Exhibit 1.8a enhance literacy leadership practices and enable students to make better life decisions. They increase student comprehension, not for reading assignments alone, but across disciplines, throughout grades, and into students' lives. As Hattie explains, it is important for teaching and learning to have "directive, activating, and involved *sets of actions* and content . . . so that learning can be monitored, feedback provided, and information given when learning is successful" (2009, p. 37). Yet, a literacy action is not a generic flotation device. These literacy actions do not replace and are not in addition to state standards, but are essential, rigorous components of standards at all levels.

> A literacy action is not a generic flotation device.

In support of the conclusion by Reeves (2009, p. 119) that "Administrators can walk marathons through the hallways and classrooms of a school and accomplish nothing if they do not begin with a clear and consistent idea of what effective instruction looks like and have the ability to communicate the elements of effective instruction in clear and unmistakable terms," each literacy action is framed around four instructionally explicit components that support the Common Core Standards, assessments, and curricular expectations.

Guidelines for Using the Literacy Action Frameworks for Instruction

The following section transports literacy instruction into the 21st century by connecting the critical thinking needed in different disciplines (Chapter 2) with life examples. Classroom Student Activities (which may be copied) guide adolescent citizen journalist actions. Each literacy action framework includes the following components (*analyzing* is the literacy action used in the following examples):

1. **What does *analyzing* look like? Why is analyzing an important 21st-century skill?** In this section, a relevant true story provides an example of a real-life application of each literacy action, followed by an application question to stimulate dialogue. This section lifts instruction outside the four walls of school to understand what thinking *during* life looks like, whether it is by other adolescents, heroes, or presidents. The informational student texts reflect qualitative text complexity elements as identified in the Common Core Standards.

2. **What is *analyzing*?** In this section, an in-depth definition is followed by a "student-friendly" definition for differentiation. It is important to note the real-life application precedes the traditional definition to balance surface information with deep learning. This provides students opportunities to actively construct their understanding.

3. **As a result of *analyzing*, what will *learners* understand, be able to do, and explore to improve the quality of their 21st-century lives?** In this section, examples of how to naturally integrate *analyzing* into instruction are included. An example from the Common Core State Standards for the disciplines of math, reading/writing, history, and science is included in this section to demonstrate the alignment with explicit instruction.

4. **As a result of *analyzing*, what will 21st-century *leaders* understand, be able to do, and explore?** Explicit literacy leadership connections (Chapter 3) are established in this section.

5. **Student Activity for *analyzing*:** An explicit, aligned literacy activity, designed for students to construct their understanding, supports teachers in transferring the literacy action directly into their instruction.

Literacy Action Instructional Frameworks

 EXHIBIT 1.8a **Literacy Action Frameworks**

Analyzing

What does *analyzing* look like?

Why is *analyzing* an important 21st-century literacy life skill?

On August 5, 2010, a Chilean mine collapsed, trapping 33 miners. Since they were trapped more than 2,000 feet below the surface and a long way from the mine entrance, finding the men would be a challenge. And drilling a rescue shaft to reach miners who were trapped so deeply was an unprecedented challenge. The chief engineer, Andres Sougarret, began with maps of the mine and assembled a team of 300 people to participate in the search and rescue effort. The team talked with the men who were the last to make it out of the mine before the collapse. The team also had to determine exactly what "collapsed" meant in this particular situation. After riding into the mine, it was determined that the cave-in brought down 700,000 tons of rock. Drilling through this could create a second collapse, so the decision was made to drill a new shaft. The team analyzed all available information to estimate where the men were trapped and the best method to rescue them. Seventeen days after the collapse, the rescue team found a note attached to the drill when it was brought to the surface stating that all 33 miners were alive. Knowing the location of the miners, the engineer determined that three plans were needed, each with different methods for drilling. Plans A, B, and C were enacted simultaneously. The Chilean Navy and United States NASA engineers collaborated on the design of the rescue capsule, named Phoenix. More than two months later, all 33 men made it to the surface—alive!

Describe how incorporating the literacy action of *analyzing* helps us respond to unexpected life events.

_____

_____

_____

_____

What is *analyzing*?

Being able to analyze information is a vital skill, due to the increasing availability of unfiltered information. Analyzing requires the learner and leader to examine the information by breaking it into component parts and determine how the parts relate to one another, and to the purpose, in order to acquire meaning. Analyzing includes being able to consider, determine what something consists of, investigate, break complex things into simpler parts, study relationships, and identify parts.

EXHIBIT 1.8a   **Literacy Action Frameworks** *(continued)*

"Student-friendly" terms for differentiating the meaning of *analyzing:* to examine, to find out what something is made of, to think about the whole in terms of its parts.

As a result of *analyzing*, what will learners understand, be able to do, and explore to improve the quality of their 21st-century lives?

Analyzing is a whole-to-part approach to learning. It is incorporated when students identify the parts of the whole and their relationship to one another. Analysis begins with the whole unit and breaks it down into parts. Examples of students successfully applying *analyzing* include students being able to edit their writing and being able to determine fact from fiction while reading.

Common Core State Standards example for math: Analyze and solve linear equations and pairs of simultaneous linear equations. Solve real-world and mathematical problems leading to two linear equations in two variables. (Math, p. 54, Gr. 8, No. 8-a)

As a result of *analyzing*, what will 21st-century leaders understand, be able to do, and explore?

Leaders analyze how elements and components are aligned to efficiently and effectively achieve stated goals, drive the mission, and measure progress to fulfill the stated vision for the organization.

Leaders must become directly involved in the analysis of the outcomes occurring as a result of the implementation of the prescribed actions. As results of these actions are gathered, leaders make the results explicit to members of the group. Leaders who lack courage often discount results that did not meet or attain the stated goals. Leaders unwilling to or lacking the courage to share the findings of the implementation actions can eventually lose their credibility as leaders. During the analysis of data, effective leaders do not draw conclusions, but continue to ask refining, penetrating, and probing questions to generate participant reflection regarding the appropriateness and effectiveness of the process, products, and actions of the implementation design.

Leaders do not analyze the results of the implementation process for the purpose of evaluating the actions of the participants, but for the purpose of improving member performance and preparing for the next round of implementation actions. It is the *process* that is being evaluated and assessed. The participants are provided with support, resources, and suggestions for increasing their capacity to improve the implementation design. Incorporating *analyzing* into the Disciplined Practice model for leadership is not for the purpose of evaluation, but for the purpose of developing accountability.

EXHIBIT 1.8a **Literacy Action Frameworks** *(continued)*

Student Activity for *analyzing:*

Learning Objective: You will be able to identify and use **analyzing** to read complex text and specific words and phrases with independence and confidence.

Real-Life Example of Analyzing:

On August 5, 2010, a Chilean mine collapsed, trapping 33 miners. Since they were trapped more than 2,000 feet below the surface and a long way from the mine entrance, finding the men would be a challenge. And drilling a rescue shaft to reach miners who were trapped so deeply was an unprecedented challenge. The chief engineer, Andres Sougarret, began with maps of the mine and assembled a team of 300 people to participate in the search and rescue effort. The team talked with the men who were the last to make it out of the mine before the collapse. The team also had to determine exactly what "collapsed" meant in this particular situation. After riding into the mine, it was determined that the cave-in brought down 700,000 tons of rock. Drilling through this could create a second collapse, so the decision was made to drill a new shaft. The team analyzed all available information to estimate where the men were trapped and the best method to rescue them. Seventeen days after the collapse, the rescue team found a note attached to the drill when it was brought to the surface. All 33 miners were alive.

Knowing the location of the miners, the engineer determined that three plans were needed, each with different methods for drilling. Plans A, B, and C were enacted simultaneously. The Chilean Navy and United States NASA engineers collaborated on the design of the rescue capsule, named Phoenix. More than two months later, all 33 men made it to the surface—alive!

What is *Analyzing*? To examine, to find out what something is made of, to think about the whole as its parts.

Questions:

1. Describe how the effective use of **analyzing** by the engineer and his team contributed to the safe return of the miners.

2. Explain how you use **analyzing** in your daily life.

3. How does **analyzing** help differentiate fact from inaccurate information when doing research?

EXHIBIT
1.8a
Literacy Action Frameworks *(continued)*

Applying

What does *applying* look like?

Why is *applying* a 21st-century literacy life skill?

One of the more advanced and often misunderstood examples of the literacy action of applying relates to the National Football League.
When watching professional football on Sunday afternoons, the casual observer cannot begin to comprehend the literacy actions required of coaches and announcers. From the sideline, to the coaches' booth above the stadium, to the announcers broadcasting the play-by-play, all communication must be understood, analyzed, and acted upon in a matter of seconds from inception to completion. The degree and level of the literacy action of applying needed to select a play and transfer it to the sideline coaches, who then electronically and visually communicate it to the players on the field, is extensive. Players and coaches rehearse, practice, refine, and hone plays for weeks to prepare for one specific game situation. The act of choosing and successfully communicating one play out of the hundreds of plays that have been drawn up, run through, selected just for this game, and applied to a specific player and defensive situation reflects the true essence of applying.

Once the play is being run, applying is used by announcers and photographers. Announcers offer a moment-by-moment description of the action, then electronically replay it. Sideline photographers begin using applying to dissect and second-guess the skills, blocking patterns, defensive sets, man-to-man match-ups, and split-second decisions that either ensured or doomed the success of the play. The literacy action of applying is complicated and beautiful at the same time. Incorporating the literacy action of applying into one's Disciplined Practice requires intentionality.

Describe how coaches incorporate multiple literacy actions prior to taking full advantage of the *applying* literacy action.

_____

_____

_____

When a football play is not successful, what particular literacy actions may not have been thoroughly enacted?

_____

EXHIBIT 1.8a **Literacy Action Frameworks** *(continued)*

What is *applying*?

Applying is using a rule, knowledge, or information, usually in a new way. Applying includes being able to: implement, demonstrate, dramatize, employ, illustrate, interpret, operate, schedule, sketch, or concentrate hard.

"Student-friendly" terms for differentiating the meaning of *applying*: to do something, use, write, solve, practice, put into service, make work for a purpose.

As a result of *applying*, what will learners understand, be able to do, and explore to improve the quality of their 21st-century lives?

Learners who apply information are able to directly use concepts to achieve an outcome. Applying extends beyond knowing information to transferring it into knowledge through usage. Learners typically act on knowledge when they believe it will be successful. Learners will be able to gather information from several sources (Web, presentation tools, Elluminate sessions) and use it in a research project. Feedback on mistakes will be integrated and applied to the next lesson.

Common Core State Standards example for math: Apply and extend previous understandings of arithmetic to algebraic expressions. Evaluate expressions at specific values of their variables. (Math, p. 43, Gr. 6, No. 6EE-c)

As a result of *applying*, what will 21st-century leaders understand, be able to do, and explore?

Leaders who incorporate the literacy action of *applying* into their Disciplined Practice perform three very specific actions. First, they facilitate participant interactions. Leaders who support interactions gather information, apply that information to build consensus, and develop trust between and within groups. Second, leaders encourage participants to think outside their normal roles and responsibilities by asking probing questions. These questions churn rich dialogue that focuses on applying solutions rather than being paralyzed by challenges. Finally, leaders create an environment of opportunity where participants are encouraged to take risks, empowered to make predictions, and expected to honestly and critically present their failures and successes to stretch the group's ability to learn and understand by applying their lessons-learned to new areas.

EXHIBIT 1.8a   **Literacy Action Frameworks** *(continued)*

Student Activity for *applying:*

Learning Objective: You will be able to identify and use **applying** to read complex text and specific words and phrases with independence and confidence.

Real-Life Example of Applying:

When watching professional football on Sunday afternoons, the casual observer cannot begin to comprehend the communications which occur between coaches and players. From the sideline, to the coaches' booth above the stadium, to the announcers broadcasting the play-by-play, all communication must be clear, explicit, and actionable in a matter of seconds.

Coaches in the booth above the field select and send the next play to coaches on the sideline, who electronically, visually, or manually communicate with players on the field. Precise skills and hours of practice are required to make this type of communication possible. Players and coaches rehearse, practice, refine, and hone plays for weeks to prepare for the one specific game situation when the chances of a particular play's success are greatest.

One play must be chosen out of hundreds of plays that have been drawn up, run through, and selected just for this game. One play must be chosen that was designed for a specific player or a precise defensive situation. One play, when not communicated clearly, may mean the difference in winning or losing the game.

What is *Applying*? To do something, use, write, solve, practice, put into service, make work for a purpose.

Questions:

1. Describe how **applying** is used during football games.

2. Explain how you use **applying** in your daily life.

3. How does **applying** help you solve equations in math class?

EXHIBIT 1.8a **Literacy Action Frameworks** (continued)

Creating

What does *creating* look like?

Why is *creating* a 21st-century literacy life skill?

In response to presidential election results that were disputed by a significant number of citizens, an uprising began throughout Iran. To prevent the world from finding out about the serious level of dissent, the Iranian leadership silenced opposition by shutting down Internet service. Because they prevented all communication with the outside world (Daragahi, 2009), it appeared that the new leadership had succeeded in squelching the uprising.

Creating became the important real-time literacy skill as citizens revolted against government control of all communication. Cell phone photographs and social networking communication became the only forms of contact from within Iran. News outlets were faced with a dilemma. Network news stations, including CNN, began adopting different standards for confirming accuracy and reliability in order to include information gathered by Iranian citizen journalists in their newscasts. Viewers of CNN experienced network standards changing in real time, and publicly. Newscasters announced that it was decided that unsubstantiated photos, not verified as authentic, would be used to report the news about Iran. Given the dire situation, networks displayed written statements explaining that unverifiable cell phone photos were being included in newscasts because they were the only source of communication as the result of the crackdown within Iran.

The skill of creating was used by the citizen journalists as they risked their lives while desperately communicating the uprising to the outside world with their cell phones. And creating was also evident in news stations, as they adapted traditional core standards to the new situation to enable the story of Iran's grim literacy clampdown to be communicated. The world was audience to the evolving skill of creating.

How did CNN use *creating* to resolve the conflict between the mandate of accurate reporting and the demands of an information crisis? What other literacy actions were evident?

_____

_____

_____

_____

EXHIBIT 1.8a   **Literacy Action Frameworks** *(continued)*

What is *creating*?

Creating is generating a new, original idea, product, or point of view. It causes something to happen or exist. It is putting component parts together to make a whole. Creating is when learners or leaders synthesize components, stimulated by questioning, resulting in new concepts, thoughts, or patterns.

Creating includes being able to: refine, produce, assemble, construct, design, develop an original idea, adapt, formulate, invent, refine, and cause something to happen.

"Student-friendly" terms for differentiating the meaning of *creating*: to present a new idea, to cause to happen, to write, to invent, to use something in a new way.

As a result of *creating*, what will learners understand, be able to do, and explore to improve the quality of their 21st-century lives?

Creating produces outcomes that include composing a new piece of writing, inventing a product, designing an original idea, and developing a new piece of software. Publishing, both on the Web, as in blogging, and in more traditional media, requires creating. Developing a new character through acting, writing a story, painting a picture, choreographing a dance, or writing the music or lyrics of a new song is creating.

Common Core State Standards example for math: Create equations in two or more variables to represent relationships between quantities. (Math, p. 65, High School)

As a result of *creating*, what will 21st-century leaders understand, be able to do, or explore?

Creating requires the leader to be open and accepting of multiple data points, divergent opinions, and different ideas. Data, opinions, and ideas fuel creating. Creating results in new ideas and unique ways of solving problems. Today, more than ever, leaders must be creative. Leaders use creating to lead, guide, and direct everyone with whom they work to develop and practice creativity within themselves.

Leaders who are creative understand not only what is to be produced, but also how to achieve this goal with the least amount of effort, energy, and resources. Leaders dispense credit for the success of the organization to the participants. The better they achieve their goals, the less they are acknowledged for their leadership, because they make it look easy. Creating successful facilitation of the work of the organization is the goal of the leader. Creative leaders know and understand that together we can and alone we won't.

EXHIBIT 1.8a **Literacy Action Frameworks** *(continued)*

Student Activity for *creating:*

Learning Objective: You will be able to identify and use **creating** to read complex text and specific words and phrases with independence and confidence.

Real-Life Example of Creating:

In response to presidential election results that were disputed by a significant number of Iranians, an uprising began throughout Iran. To prevent the world from finding out about the serious level of dissent, the Iranian leadership silenced opposition by shutting down Internet service. Because they prevented all communication with the outside world (Daragahi, 2009), it appeared that the new leadership had succeeded in squelching the uprising.

Creating became the real-time literacy skill as citizens revolted against government control of all communication. Cell phone photographs and social networking communication became the only forms of contact from within Iran.

News outlets were faced with a dilemma. Network news stations, including CNN, began adopting different standards for confirming accuracy and reliability in order to include information gathered by Iranian citizen journalists in their newscasts. Viewers of CNN experienced network standards changing in real time, and publicly. Newscasters announced that it was decided that unsubstantiated photos, not verified as authentic, would be used to report the news about Iran. Given the dire situation, networks displayed written statements explaining that unverifiable cell phone photos were being included in newscasts because they were the only source of communication as the result of the crackdown within Iran.

What is *Creating*? To do something, use, write, solve, practice, put into service, make work for a purpose.

Questions:

1. Describe how **creating** contributed to helping people during this crisis.

2. Explain how you can use **creating** in your daily life.

3. How is **creating** different in English classes compared to science classes?

EXHIBIT 1.8a **Literacy Action Frameworks** *(continued)*

Evaluating

What does *evaluating* look like?

Why is *evaluating* a 21st-century literacy life skill?

We were sitting on our deck one evening when, from the raging Shenandoah River 600 feet below, we heard young voices yelling "9-1-1." Hearing their faint pleas, we dialed the emergency number. Soon, our deck became the command post for coordinating communication among the fire and rescue squad, hostage and evacuation assistance team, railroad personnel, and rescue helicopters that responded. The lives of 10 children and two adults hung in the balance; their last particles of hope were the edges of the river rocks they grasped as the powerful river pulled at their weakened bodies. What was the lifeline connecting their panicked voices to the helicopter's rescue baskets? The victims' decision to simultaneously yell "9-1-1" rather than randomly shouting the less discriminate call of "help" allowed their voices to permeate the thunderous sound of the waterfalls and cross the distance up the mountain into the consciousness of our quiet Sunday evening on the deck.

An article about the incident described it as "a miracle rescue" (Marshall, 2009). The miracle of this rescue stemmed from the evaluation skills of the helicopter pilot. Although he was in a precarious situation himself, hovering above the falls, the pilot provided a strong voice of reason, as he demanded the information necessary for appropriate actions. "We need to be accountable," he calmly said through the speaker for all standing in the safety of the command post to hear. "How many people need to be rescued? Let me be perfectly clear. Did the child who was hanging from the rock make it to safety?" While operating the treacherous nighttime rescue just above the falls between Blue Ridge Mountain peaks, the pilot's voice equaled the power of his searchlight as he calmly and steadfastly demonstrated evaluation skills that appraised the situation and selected next steps that would result in the safe rescue of all 10 children and both adults.

In what ways did the pilot's ability to *evaluate* the precarious nighttime rescue contribute to saving all the children?

_____

_____

_____

EXHIBIT 1.8a **Literacy Action Frameworks** *(continued)*

Describe the importance of the evaluation skills displayed by the children and two adults.

_____

_____

_____

How do they compare?

_____

_____

What is *evaluating*?

To evaluate is to take a stand or make a decision based on available information. It is the learner or leader's ability to appraise a situation, then make a choice based on standards. Evaluating is an attempt to increase understanding. Evaluation is applied to research. Evaluating includes being able to: argue, appraise, assess, conclude, coordinate, critique, discriminate, justify, prioritize, rank, recommend, make a judgment, fix a value, and weigh evidence.

"Student-friendly" terms for differentiating the meaning of *evaluating*: check, support, understand, question.

As a result of *evaluating*, what will learners understand, be able to do, and explore to improve the quality of their 21st-century lives?

To evaluate is to consider criteria to make a decision. Evaluation includes being able to justify the decision by providing solid support and/or a defense of the decision. Examples of evaluating include participating in a debate, determining appropriate information to include in a composition, and designing a plan for a project. Also, evaluating is a particularly vital life skill for adolescents, because they are faced with personal, life-threatening choices that have to be made while they are enduring peer pressure.

Common Core State Standards example for history; social studies in reading: Evaluate an author's premises, claims, and evidence by corroborating or challenging them with other information. (ELA, p. 19, Gr. 11-12, No. 8)

EXHIBIT 1.8a **Literacy Action Frameworks** *(continued)*

As a result of *evaluating*, what will 21st-century leaders understand, be able to do, and explore?

Leaders who incorporate evaluating into their Disciplined Practice will be able to appraise any situation after collecting all the appropriate information. Determining appropriate steps, leaders will make decisions by selecting actions that support the intended outcome and result in satisfactory resolutions. Leaders possess the capacity to act.

During the four-hour Shenandoah rescue, leadership changed hands many times as the situation evolved and more information was gathered. Yet, it was the pilot's capacity to evaluate that provided the strongest leadership among the collective brave group. The ability to lead is demonstrated by a person's ability to evaluate the situation by stepping up and assuming command or standing down and accepting directions. Leaders evaluate situations and take personal actions that demonstrate their ability to lead, follow, or step out of the way, as dictated by the situation.

EXHIBIT 1.8a **Literacy Action Frameworks** *(continued)*

Student Activity for *evaluating*:

Learning Objective: You will be able to identify and use **evaluating** to read complex text and specific words and phrases with independence and confidence.

Real-Life Example of Evaluating:

From the raging Shenandoah River, young voices could be heard yelling "9-1-1." A phone call was made to alert officials, and a newspaper article the following day described "a miracle rescue" of 10 children and two adults. The miracle of this rescue stemmed from the skills and actions of the helicopter pilot. Although he was in a precarious situation himself, hovering above the water in the darkness, the pilot provided a strong voice of reason, as he demanded the information necessary for appropriate actions. "We need to be accountable," he calmly said through the speaker for all standing in the safety of the command post to hear. "How many people need to be rescued? Let me be perfectly clear. Did the child who was hanging from the rock make it to safety?" While operating the treacherous nighttime rescue just above the falls between Blue Ridge Mountain peaks, the pilot's voice equaled the power of his searchlight as he calmly and steadfastly conducted the operation that would result in the safe rescue of all 10 children and both adults.

What is *Evaluating*? To check, support, understand, question.

Questions:

1. Describe how **evaluating** was used in this successful rescue.

2. Explain how you use **evaluating** in your daily life.

3. How does **evaluating** determine the effectiveness of your laboratory reports in science?

EXHIBIT 1.8a **Literacy Action Frameworks** *(continued)*

Exploring

What does *exploring* look like?

Why is *exploring* a 21st-century literacy life skill?

The Deepwater Horizon drilling rig exploded on April 20, 2010, triggering the largest marine oil spill accident in the history of the industry. BP stopped the flow of oil three months later. Several previous attempts to stop the spill, and some of the efforts to minimize the human and economic impact of the catastrophe, had failed, while the world watched in frustration.

How much farther into the 21st century will we need to be before we recognize that limited thinking born out of past eras is not sufficient? Trying to resolve new problems with old solutions is likely to be as ineffective in education as it was in the failed attempts to deal with the Deepwater Horizon disaster. Can thinking born out of past eras, limited to 20th-century issues, meet today's needs?

Life exists in a new orbit. Not only has technology paved the way for the global economy, social and cultural reactions are establishing deep changes. Bloom's taxonomy prepared students well for 20th-century thinking. Today, additional types of thought, such as exploring new possibilities, are demanded to resolve problems of enormous complexity.

Inside this orbit of 21st-century experiences demanding thinking that can explore new possibilities, BP has much company. For the first time in its 96-year history, the Federal Reserve Bank of New York is foreclosing on homes. These challenges, when combined with economic situations such as deflation, a condition most people have never before experienced, increase awareness of problems awaiting solutions requiring literacy actions such as exploring.

How can we prepare students to live responsible lives as problem-solvers able to explore different types of thought? What thought patterns have yet to be discovered?

_____

_____

_____

EXHIBIT 1.8a   **Literacy Action Frameworks** *(continued)*

Predict ways *exploring* will continue to increase in necessity throughout the 21st century.

_____

_____

_____

What is *exploring*?

To explore is to be aware of your mistakes, learn from mistakes, determine the nature of a problem, investigate, inquire, examine, probe, and canvass.

"Student-friendly" terms for differentiating the meaning of *exploring*: search, find out, look into, learn beyond the lesson, think carefully and decide so you can find out more about something, be able to research.

As a result of *exploring*, what will learners understand, be able to do, and explore to improve the quality of their 21st-century lives?

To explore is to make a mistake, then take a step to learn from it. Mistakes can be concrete objects that were formed incorrectly, or results not substantiated by data. Frequently, mistakes are errors in decisions or thinking. An example of exploring includes completing a history assignment then continuing reading on the topic to answer questions that were not posed in the assignment.

Common Core State Standards example for writing: Use technology, including the Internet, to produce and publish writing and present the relationships between information and ideas efficiently as well as to interact and collaborate with others. (ELA, p. 43, Gr. 8, No. 6)

As a result of *exploring*, what will 21st-century leaders understand, be able to do, and explore?

For leadership, exploring is the process used to keep improvement on track and focused upon the adopted goals and predicted formative improvement data. Exploring occurs when the data from the formative stage of the improvement is collected through conversations with participants to determine how, at this moment in time, participants believe themselves and the goals to be performing. Exploring supports the leader and participants in making decisions at critical points when it becomes apparent goals are not going to be achieved. Leaders support teams as they revisit data and explore options based on new learnings from mistakes, errors, or predictions that require adjustment as data unfolds.

EXHIBIT 1.8a **Literacy Action Frameworks** *(continued)*

Student Activity for *exploring:*

Learning Objective: You will be able to identify and use **exploring** to read complex text and specific words and phrases with independence and confidence.

Real-Life Example of Exploring:

The Deepwater Horizon drilling rig exploded on April 20, 2010, triggering the largest marine oil spill accident in the history of the industry. BP stopped the flow of oil three months later. Several previous attempts to stop the spill, and some of the efforts to minimize the human and economic impact of the catastrophe, had failed, while the world watched in frustration.

In this case, limited thinking born out of past eras was not sufficient. Trying to resolve new problems with old solutions is often not effective. Thinking born out of past eras, limited to 20th-century issues, cannot always meet today's needs.

What is *Exploring*? To search, to find out, look into, learn beyond the lesson, to think carefully and decide so you can find out more about something, be able to research.

Questions:

1. Describe how **exploring** could have been more effectively used in this example.

2. Explain how you use **exploring** in your daily life.

3. How has the need for **exploring** increased over the last ten years?

EXHIBIT 1.8a   **Literacy Action Frameworks** (continued)

Inferring

What does *inferring* look like?

Why is *inferring* a 21st-century literacy life skill?

On September 14, 2001, three days after the terrorist attacks of September 11, President George W. Bush, speaking from the ruins of the World Trade Center towers, said, "I can hear you. The rest of the world hears you. And the people who knocked these buildings down will hear all of us soon."

Leaders draw upon inferences when acting in a very decisive manner. The directedness of experienced leaders in times of crisis is observed through their deliberate, thoughtful, and reflective manner. Inference is often obscure and subtle. President Bush, after the September 11 tragedy, visited the site of the World Trade Towers in lower Manhattan. Standing amid the rubble, he made the above statement, indicating that this act of violence would not go unanswered.

The president relied on the ability of U.S. citizens to infer from his remarks that the United States of America, and the world, would not stand for this type of unprovoked violence. The people who heard the remarks inferred that this country would stand firm and take the correct next step. There were no specific plans, threats, or challenges thrown down. Through his remarks, the president implied that our nation's capacity to overcome that tragedy was unquestionable.

In what ways did the use of the literacy action of *inferring* enable the president to communicate powerfully to both Americans and terrorists?

_____

_____

_____

_____

What is *inferring*?
To infer is to decide if something is true based on available information. Inferences are conclusions drawn from evidence. For reading, inferring occurs when the reader puts together what she or he read with what he or she already knows to ask a question or draw a conclusion. The reader makes meaning from background information, personal experiences, and information implied by the author. Conclusions are not based on opinion or influenced by emotions. Making an inference is the foundation of comprehension. Inferring is necessary on a daily basis in all aspects of life, including maintaining friendships and making safe, healthy choices. Inferring includes being able to conclude and judge and make a corollary, abstract thought, or analogy.

EXHIBIT 1.8a   **Literacy Action Frameworks** *(continued)*

"Student-friendly" terms for differentiating the meaning of *inferring:* deciding, figuring out, putting things together with what you know to ask a question or make a choice.

As a result of *inferring,* **what will learners understand, be able to do, and explore to improve the quality of their 21st-century lives?**

Examples of when inferences are made include incorporating background experiences when reasoning, determining the main idea, and making judgments. Situations that require inferring include selecting articles and book titles for a research project and determining an appropriate modification or intervention to support an outcome. An example of inferring is seeing tears in someone's eyes after receiving a phone call, then immediately inquiring if they are all right.

Common Core State Standards example for reading: Cite textual evidence to support analysis of what the text says explicitly as well as inferences drawn from the text. (ELA, p. 36, Gr. 6, No. 1)

As a result of *inferring,* **what will 21st-century leaders understand, be able to do, and explore?**

Inferring demonstrates a leader's ability to insert a blend of reality and optimism into the dialogue of systemic or organizational change. It is a literacy action when delivered by a skillful leader who can draw on background information to generate commitment. Leaders in schools today guide their staff members to infer what can be accomplished without directing actions, identifying procedures, or dictating processes. Leaders who are skillful in the literacy action of inferring can bring a magnified focus on critical areas of need without determining how or when the actions will be implemented, or who will implement them. Leaders who demonstrate inferring keep participants engaged, motivated, involved, and prepared to take the right next steps to solve challenging problems, address organizational needs, or prepare for future transformational changes in the system.

EXHIBIT 1.8a   **Literacy Action Frameworks** *(continued)*

Student Activity for *inferring:*

Learning Objective: You will be able to identify and use **inferring** to read complex text and specific words and phrases with independence and confidence.

Real-Life Example of Inferring:

On September 14, 2001, three days after the terrorist attacks of September 11, President George W. Bush, speaking from the ruins of the World Trade Center towers, said, "I can hear you. The rest of the world hears you. And the people who knocked these buildings down will hear all of us soon." When President Bush made that statement, he was indicating that this act of violence would not go unanswered.

What is *Inferring*? To decide, figure out, put things together with what you know to ask a question or make a choice.

Questions:

1. Describe how the president relied on **inferring** to convey his intentions.

2. Explain how you use **inferring** in your daily life.

3. How can using **inferring** during a history discussion change your understanding about a historical text?

EXHIBIT 1.8a   Literacy Action Frameworks *(continued)*

Judging

What does *judging* look like?

Why is *judging* a 21st-century literacy life skill?

Consider how Captain Chesley "Sully" Sullenberger was able to save every life on his plane by successfully landing it in the Hudson River after losing both engines on January 15, 2009. He successfully assessed the situation, which included much unexpected incoming information—from dials to ducks. The capacity to judge information is a vital life skill.

Contrast this pilot's decisions with the many adults whose lives would not have been ruined if they had integrated several literacy actions to judge information over time prior to investing in the Bernie Madoff Ponzi scheme that decimated their savings. How was this breakdown of the fundamental literacy action of judging possible? What void created the potential for gaps in fundamental awareness? Habits of Mind such as "taking responsible risks" were not in evidence. Could the scales have so dramatically tipped if the weight of literacy actions such as judging had been used to balance the weight of the unknown?

Whether opening mail, accessing e-mail, watching television, or surfing the Internet, we must keep in mind that there are those in search of easy prey who sit like hunters comfortably perched in trees waiting for a prized eight-point buck to get too close. Firewalls are not sufficient protection against the daily onslaught of intrusions on our personal well-being, not for children or adults. Critical thinking is life's protective shield. Judging is at the core.

In what ways was the literacy action of *judging* able to guide Sully Sullenberger to the best, life-saving decision?

_____

_____

_____

Contrast Sullenberger's *judgment* capacity with that of clients who willingly provided Bernie Madoff with millions of dollars while requesting minimal or no documentation.

_____

_____

_____

EXHIBIT 1.8a **Literacy Action Frameworks** *(continued)*

What is *judging*?

Judging is the process of reaching a decision or drawing a conclusion after consideration based on evidence. It includes sensible opinion based on careful thinking and understanding. Judging includes assessing a person, situation, or event. It means to decide, settle, gauge, estimate, and approximate. Judging requires discernment.

"Student-friendly" terms for differentiating the meaning of *judging*: to understand then decide, to make a good choice, to pick something carefully.

As a result of *judging*, what will learners understand, be able to do, and explore that will improve the quality of their 21st-century lives?

Learners who incorporate judging will collect accurate evidence. This evidence will be the basis for making a decision, no matter how opinion may influence the process of judging a person, situation, or event. An example is making a judgment based on the results of a poll.

Common Core State Standards example for science in reading: Distinguish among facts, reasoned judgment based on research findings, and speculation in a text. (ELA, p. 62, Gr. 6-8, No. 8)

As a result of *judging*, what will 21st-century leaders understand, be able to do, and explore?

Leaders applying the literacy action of *judging* practice several critical management skills. First, leaders who are adept at judging performance, process, and products have the ability to slow down the implementation of the action until participants know and are able to do what they are expected to do. By slowing down the action, leaders are able to monitor and verify the level of expertise of the participants. Slowing down the action permits leaders to identify gaps in learning and provide support or correction before participants become invested in the action and create a mental model which, when followed, will not produce the desired results. Leaders who are competent in judging the performance of others understand participants are unable to immediately perform to the level of skill one would expect from an expert with more than 10,000 hours of practice (Gladwell, 2008).

Another skill leaders must possess to successfully judge performance is knowing when, where, and how to introduce participants to new levels of performance. Leaders who are competent at judging participant performance never place participants in a situation for which they are not prepared, have not received the appropriate training, or are not thoroughly briefed on what is expected of them. Participants have a clear vision of the success or the failure of the task. Leaders who judge participant performance make sure the process of judging is transparent to the participants and provide every assurance the task can and will be successfully completed.

EXHIBIT 1.8a **Literacy Action Frameworks** *(continued)*

Student Activity for *judging:*

Learning Objective: You will be able to identify and use **judging** to read complex text and specific words and phrases with independence and confidence.

Real-Life Example of Judging:

Captain Chesley "Sully" Sullenberger was able to save every life on his plane by successfully landing it in the Hudson River after losing both engines on January 15, 2009. He successfully assessed the situation, which included much unexpected incoming information—from dials to ducks. The engines of his plane had apparently come into contact with a large flock of birds (a situation called a "bird strike"), and both engines were disabled. Captain Sullenberger considered the options and decided on a water landing. He announced that passengers needed to brace themselves, then he successfully "ditched" the Airbus in the Hudson River safely. He then made sure every passenger got out of the plane safely.

What is *Judging*? Reaching a decision, assessing a situation for positive and negative information.

Questions:

1. Describe how **judging** used by the airplane pilot contributed to the positive outcome.

2. Explain how you use **judging** in your daily life.

3. What are the similarities and differences between **judging** a musical recital and judging a debate?

EXHIBIT 1.8a **Literacy Action Frameworks** *(continued)*

Monitoring

What does *monitoring* look like?

Why is *monitoring* a 21st-century literacy life skill?

While preparing for takeoff, I saw a pilot with a flashlight doing a safety check around the outside perimeter of his plane. Why would the pilot do an exterior safety check? It was not his job. An entire grounds crew was responsible for safely preparing the plane. Yet, accountability for the passengers belonged to the pilot. Just as the entire roster of passengers is the pilot's responsibility, the principal of a school has the bottom-line accountability for every student. When I was the principal of a school of 850 students, being accountable for every student required the literacy action of holding regularly scheduled conversations with every teacher about each student. These Compelling Conversations successfully provided opportunities to frequently monitor each student's progress by blurring traditional roles. Whether with a pilot's flashlight, a leader's conversations, or teacher-and-student dialogue, it is vital for monitoring to take place directly "at the coalface," where decisions are made.

In what ways does the literacy action of *monitoring* pry open traditional norms sealed off from accountability?

_____

_____

_____

What additional literacy actions increase as a result of *monitoring*?

_____

_____

_____

What is *monitoring*?
To monitor is to intentionally be aware of the current state. It is to regularly keep an eye on a situation. Frequently, information is displayed for the purpose of making a decision. As a result of monitoring, modifications can be determined.

"Student-friendly" terms for differentiating the meaning of *monitoring*: to check, compare, get information.

Common Core State Standards example for writing: With some guidance and support from peers and adults, develop and strengthen writing as needed by planning, revision, editing, rewriting or trying a new approach, focusing on how well purpose and audience have been addressed. (ELA, p. 43, Gr. 7, No. 5)

EXHIBIT 1.8a   **Literacy Action Frameworks** *(continued)*

As a result of *monitoring*, what will learners understand, be able to do, and explore that will improve the quality of their 21st-century lives?

When a student incorporates monitoring, specifically self-monitoring, improvement is possible. Monitoring progress leads to achieving goals. Examples of monitoring include monitoring during reading to determine comprehension levels, and using formative data to adjust medications.

As a result of *monitoring*, what will 21st-century leaders understand, be able to do, and explore?

Disciplined Practice requires the leader to continually monitor progress towards attainment of the specific adopted goals of the group. As plans are implemented and members take action, results are gathered. The leader does not have to monitor each of the separate resulting products produced by participant actions. However, the leader must collaboratively establish set points in the continuum of implementation where participants, typically in Data Teams, openly share the resulting progress towards the attainment of the adopted goals. Monitoring is not evaluative. Monitoring of the implementation actions requires the leader to determine how the concentric elements, components, and pieces align with and to the desired goals. Periodically, monitoring gathers specific data on a predetermined schedule to assure all participants of the team focus their individual and collective effort, energy, and resources on practices designed to provide specific data on the implementation design. The predicted benchmark outcomes provide the markers for determining progress. This monitoring provides feedback on the alignment of processes and depth of understanding.

Monitoring is a Disciplined Practice that is nonevaluative. Monitoring, when practiced openly, builds organizational honesty and confidence in the leader's capacity to lead. Participants at every level of an organization and system want to be acknowledged for their value and worth. Participants in every organization want to do what is in the best interest of the organization. Frequent monitoring of progress provides leaders with opportunities to commend progress towards goals.

EXHIBIT 1.8a   **Literacy Action Frameworks** *(continued)*

Student Activity for *monitoring:*

Learning Objective: You will be able to identify and use **monitoring** to read complex text and specific words and phrases with independence and confidence.

Real-Life Example of Monitoring:

While preparing for takeoff, I saw a pilot with a flashlight doing a safety check around the outside perimeter of his plane. Why would the pilot do an exterior safety check? It was not his job. An entire grounds crew was responsible for safely preparing the plane. Yet, accountability for the passengers belonged to the pilot.

The principal of a school is responsible for all the students' progress. Some principals meet with teachers individually to see how students are doing. Whether with a principal-teacher conversation, or teacher-and-student dialogue, it is important to frequently determine how much progress students are making so support can be provided when needed.

What is *Monitoring*? To check, compare, get information.

Questions:

1. Describe how **monitoring** was used by the principal to help students improve.

2. Explain how you use **monitoring** in your daily life.

3. How does your personal **monitoring** impact the choices you make and the grades on your report card?

EXHIBIT 1.8a **Literacy Action Frameworks** *(continued)*

Questioning

What does *questioning* look like?

Why is *questioning* a 21st-century literacy life skill?

After flying to Florida to aid her sister in supporting their fragile mother, Anna asked her sister if the doctor had diagnosed their mother with Alzheimer's disease. Her sister replied that she had not asked the doctor. She said she was afraid to hear the truth.

Anna was equally concerned about the possible reply, but she knew the question needed to be asked. She scheduled a meeting with the doctor. Upon hearing the doctor explain that their mother was experiencing the beginning stages of dementia, Anna and her sister were able to begin planning together for their mother's future needs.

Questioning is a choice. Just as this family was able to work together to provide the best support for their mother as a result of questioning, critical thinking in all disciplines is enhanced when questioning is integrated throughout instruction.

In what ways is *questioning* vital for appropriate decision making?

_____

_____

_____

What is *questioning*?

Questioning guides analysis thinking. Questions can express doubt or genuine curiosity. It is a point that needs to be discussed. Questions are an examination of a topic. Questions formed before, during, and after reading and writing are necessary for critical thinking. Questions provide clarity and stimulate additional research. "Questioning your assumptions and questioning your own decision-making are key factors in content literacy" (Gregory and Kuzmich, 2005b). Questioning includes being able to express, doubt, examine, probe, interrogate, query, and inquire.

"Student-friendly" terms for differentiating the meaning of *questioning*: ask, discuss, wonder, want to know more, want to understand better.

As a result of *questioning*, what will learners know, be able to do, and explore that will improve the quality of their 21st-century lives?

To make appropriate decisions and be effective problem solvers, learners must be able to ask questions. This allows for filling gaps between what is known and what is not known. Questioning is what is said or written to ask about a particular matter.

EXHIBIT 1.8a **Literacy Action Frameworks** *(continued)*

An example is to inquire about further information regarding a doctor's prognosis by asking targeted questions about a topic that will improve communication and understanding. Usually students and adults ask a wide range of questions, including:

From whose viewpoint are we seeing, reading, or learning?

From what angle or what perspective are we viewing this situation?

If that is true, then what might happen if . . . ?

What are some alternative solutions to this conflict?

(Costa and Kallick, 2008)

Common Core State Standards example for science: Evaluate the hypothesis, data, analysis, and conclusions in a science or technical text, verifying the data when possible and corroborating or challenging conclusions with other sources of information. (ELA, p. 62, Gr. 11-12, No. 8)

As a result of *questioning*, what will 21st-century leaders understand, be able to do, and explore?

A leader will be able to design effective and efficient actions when all possible alternatives are discussed. Leaders who are effective are capable of accessing the depth of participant knowledge and practice by asking five questions. This practice is often referred to as the "Five Whys." Leaders who practice asking participants "why" five times usually are able to identify the knowledge and logical progression of thought used to address a problem, and how specific actions are impacted or are predicted to impact pending results. The skill a leader possesses for framing and posing salient questions about the implementation actions determines the participants' ability to bring meaning, apply new knowledge, and create new understandings. Leaders who hone their ability to question do not need to control, direct, or dictate members' actions. Leaders who know what, how, why, when, and where members will implement actions can identify gaps in understanding that, if implemented, would result in unexpected consequences.

The Disciplined Practice of *questioning* is typically not utilized to its potential. Leaders often underutilize questioning because they believe their position and authority is derived from their ability to be decisive and directive. Rather than questioning participant actions for the purpose of identifying faulty logic, learning gaps, or lack of understanding, leaders evaluate results, direct changes, and then send participants off without building their capacity to lead their team or learn from the experience. At times, leaders may intentionally avoid asking courageous questions to delay dealing with inevitable problems. Slower is faster—we must take time to ask the hard questions to build capacity to learn in each and every participant.

 **EXHIBIT 1.8a** **Literacy Action Frameworks** *(continued)*

Student Activity for *questioning:*

Learning Objective: You will be able to identify and use **questioning** to read complex text and specific words and phrases with independence and confidence.

Real-Life Example of Questioning:

After flying to Florida to aid her sister in supporting their fragile mother, Anna asked her sister if the doctor had diagnosed their mother with Alzheimer's disease. Her sister replied that she had not asked the doctor. She said she was afraid to hear the truth.

Anna was equally concerned about the possible reply, but she knew the question needed to be asked. She scheduled a meeting with the doctor. Upon hearing the doctor explain that their mother was experiencing the beginning stages of dementia, Anna and her sister were able to begin planning together for their mother's future needs.

What is Questioning? To check, compare, get information, get better.

Questions:

1. Describe how **questioning** was used to improve the quality of a family member's life.

2. Explain how you use **questioning** in your daily life.

3. How can **questioning** in your classes improve your thinking, increase your knowledge, and improve your grades?

EXHIBIT 1.8a **Literacy Action Frameworks** *(continued)*

Synthesizing

What does *synthesizing* look like?

Why is *synthesizing* a 21st-century literacy life skill?

Amidst the chaos of the February 2010 earthquake in Chile and resulting tsunami, social networking provided an avenue for self-organizing that increased safety and saved lives. Although the 8.8 magnitude earthquake disrupted other forms of communication, Facebook and Twitter were still able to function. What occurred during this moment of crisis depicted, with mighty power, the enormous energy igniting the current literacy explosion. Simultaneously, the crisis stimulated the enormous potential of the literacy action synthesizing, as evidenced in the following two examples:

1. CNN reported and demonstrated how Google had, early on in the crisis, created technology in response: A virtual mouse was created within the Google Internet page for the "Chile earthquake" link. This unique mouse could be moved vertically, inside the link, to immediately access various emergency information. Time that would have been wasted surfing the Web was eliminated, since emergency information was synthesized into the small internal space, accessed by the newly developed mouse that simply appeared on the screen.

2. Also reported and demonstrated on CNN during this crisis was the fact that a social networker on Twitter created a hashtag, #hitsunami, as a way to create space on the Internet for synthesizing emergency information in real time. The social networkers guided one another and Internet traffic to helpful information. Communication included, "Safeway is beginning to run out of bottled water." "Gas lines at 7-11 are blocks long." "Go to this site for evacuation maps."

Both ingenious solutions were stimulated by the need to quickly synthesize and communicate crisis information. It appeared that government agencies still have much to learn about crisis management from the synthesizing abilities of citizen journalists.

In what ways does the literacy action of *synthesis* provide potential vital for meeting 21st-century needs?

_____

_____

_____

EXHIBIT 1.8a **Literacy Action Frameworks** *(continued)*

What is *synthesizing*?

Synthesizing is the combining or mixing of different ideas, facts, or experiences. These are combined to create a single idea or impression. It is figuring out how different parts can become a whole. Various parts are considered, and then synthesizing is applied as information is taken from different sources, evaluated, and connected to create understanding. Synthesizing is increasing in importance because the amount of information available is doubling every two to three years (Gardner, 2008, p. 46). It is a powerful process that establishes important connections and meaning. Synthesis responds to concerns and leads to questions and expanding knowledge.

"Student-friendly" terms for differentiating the meaning of *synthesizing*: mixing, pulling together, fitting together, thinking and then deciding.

As a result of *synthesizing*, what will learners understand, be able to do, and explore that will improve the quality of their 21st-century lives?

Students and adult learners who synthesize are able to establish connections between different ideas from multiple sources to respond to a need. Synthesizing can lead to new understandings. It can result in fresh questions being generated. When questions result, synthesis merges into the literacy action of creating. An example of synthesizing is reading several texts at one time, combining the information with a problem in current events, and creating a resolution.

Common Core State Standards example for science in reading: Synthesize information from a range of sources into a coherent understanding of a process, phenomenon, or concept, resolving conflicting information when possible. (ELA, p. 62, Gr. 11-12, No. 9)

As a result of *synthesizing*, what will 21st-century leaders understand, be able to do, and explore?

Leaders applying the literacy action of *synthesizing* oversee the process of data analysis. Synthesizing requires data in order to produce results. Synthesizing identifies what worked as predicted and what did not work. Synthesizing uses the data produced from monitoring procedures, formative assessment data, and summative assessment data to distill quantitative and qualitative data for the purpose of constructing the story behind the numbers. The construction of the story clarifies how the results either succeeded or failed to address the adopted goals. Synthesizing produces a description of identified gaps, overlaps, or breakdowns in the process of improvement with either detailed explanations or more questions to consider when planning for the next improvement cycle.

EXHIBIT 1.8a **Literacy Action Frameworks** *(continued)*

Student Activity for *synthesizing:*

Learning Objective: You will be able to identify and use **synthesizing** to read complex text and specific words and phrases with independence and confidence.

Real-Life Example of Synthesizing:

Amidst the chaos of the February 2010 earthquake in Chile and resulting tsunami, social networking provided an avenue for self-organizing that increased safety and saved lives. Although the 8.8 magnitude earthquake disrupted other forms of communication, Facebook and Twitter were still able to function. What occurred during this moment of crisis depicted, with mighty power, the enormous energy igniting the current literacy explosion. Simultaneously, the crisis stimulated the enormous potential of the literacy action synthesizing, as evidenced in the following two examples:

1. CNN reported and demonstrated how Google had, early on in the crisis, created technology in response: A virtual mouse was created within the Google Internet page for the "Chile earthquake" link. This unique mouse could be moved vertically, inside the link, to immediately access various emergency information. Time that would have been wasted surfing the Web was eliminated, since emergency information was synthesized into the small internal space, accessed by the newly developed mouse that simply appeared on the screen.

2. Also reported and demonstrated on CNN during this crisis was the fact that a social networker on Twitter created a hashtag, #hitsunami, as a way to create space on the Internet for synthesizing emergency information in real time. The social networkers guided one another and Internet traffic to helpful information. Communication included, "Safeway is beginning to run out of bottled water." "Gas lines at 7-11 are blocks long." "Go to this site for evacuation maps."

What is *Synthesizing?* To mix, pull together, fit together, think and then decide.

Questions:

1. Describe how **synthesizing** was used in this example to help people in a crisis.

2. Explain how you use **synthesizing** in your daily life.

3. How does **synthesizing** improve your knowledge of social studies and history?

EXHIBIT 1.8a   **Literacy Action Frameworks** *(continued)*

Understanding

What does *understanding* look like?

Why is *understanding* a 21st-century literacy life skill?

Natalia intently read from her iPod. When she glanced up, I asked, "Do you enjoy reading your iPod more than a traditional book?" The long flight we were on evoked a desire in most passengers to read. I observed with great interest the variety of reading modes. Natalia explained, "In the Ukraine, a book costs $50. Household incomes average $200 monthly." I quickly estimated the comparative cost of a book if it were one-fourth of my monthly income, then envisioned bare bookshelves throughout our home. Natalia continued, "I love the feel of a book. I love how it smells. I read online books because they are free."

Natalia's comments froze my thoughts. Technology is influencing learning with its relevancy and speed, but in unpredictable economic times, "free" matters even more. From the flattened world rose understanding about the changing face of literacy.

How is *understanding* a duel responsibility: first, to be able to share ideas, and then to comprehend deeply to build the basis for future knowledge?

What is *understanding*?
Understanding is the ability to explain ideas or concepts. It is knowing why or how something works, or what it means. It includes describing a situation, and knowing the meaning of an action. Understanding includes being able to: comprehend, classify, identify, recognize, select, translate, and paraphrase.

"Student-friendly" terms for differentiating the meaning of *understanding*:
to know why or how, share, report, explain, describe.

EXHIBIT 1.8a **Literacy Action Frameworks** *(continued)*

As a result of *understanding*, what will learners understand, be able to do, and explore that will improve the quality of their 21st-century lives?

Demonstrating understanding is explaining meaning generated from multiple types of media. Understanding is knowing and being able to explain that an event took place, and to determine why it occurred. An example of understanding is when customers understood the nature of the mechanical malfunctions that caused Toyota to recall a large number of vehicles recently. Because they understood the acceleration problem that might occur, customers were better prepared for that possible crisis, which may have resulted in fewer lives being lost.

Common Core State Standards example for math: Understand the connections between proportional relationships, lines, and linear equations. (Math, p. 54, Gr. 8, No. 8)

As a result of *understanding*, what will 21st-century leaders understand, be able to do, and explore?

Leaders gather knowledge from inside and outside of their organizations for the purpose of establishing new processes and procedures to improve efficiency, conserve resources, and enhance operational performance. The creation of new understanding may be best described as a marriage. Sometimes old, new, borrowed, and blue are merged and intertwined with two separate but equal functions, thus creating a new operational model. Examples of understanding include comparing informational articles, summarizing a text, completing an organizer, and using data to effectively provide clarity.

Understanding becomes operational when leaders are able to identify and define how a new entity improves performance, is resource-neutral, and makes everyone's job easier and more productive. Understanding typically results in changes. For this to happen within a system, a series of events must occur that require the leader's Disciplined Practice of the literacy action *understanding*.

EXHIBIT 1.8a   **Literacy Action Frameworks** *(continued)*

Student Activity for *understanding:*

Learning Objective: You will be able to identify and use **understanding** to read complex text and specific words and phrases with independence and confidence.

Real-Life Example of Understanding:

Natalia intently read from her iPod. When she glanced up, another airline passenger asked, "Do you enjoy reading your iPod more than a traditional book?" Natalia explained, "In the Ukraine, a book costs $50. Household incomes average $200 monthly." (Try estimating the comparative cost of a book here if it were one-fourth of your family's monthly income).

Natalia continued, "I love the feel of a book. I love how it smells. I read online books because they are free." Technology is influencing learning with its relevancy and speed, but in unpredictable economic times, "free" matters even more.

What is Understanding? To know why or how, share, report, explain, describe.

Questions:

1. Describe how Natalia's **understanding** about budgets influences her decisions.

2. Explain how you use **understanding** in your daily life.

3. How does incorporating **understanding** improve your personal decisions about purchases?

Definition resources for the "What is?" sections: *Bloom's Digital Taxonomy Map*, 2008; *Collins Cobuild Student's Dictionary*, 2005; *Differentiated Literacy Strategies*, 2005; *Engaging Classroom Assessments*, 2009; *Five Minds for the Future*, 2008; *Habits of Mind*, 2008; *Reader's Handbook*, 2002; *21st Century Skills: Rethinking How Students Learn*, 2010. Additional information about the definition resources is in the References section. Literacy actions are a synthesis from resources in Exhibit 1.6.

EXHIBIT 1.8b **Literacy Action Discussion Sheet**

Describe how incorporating _____ could help prepare *you* for unexpected changes, or improve your learning about another topic in a specific way:

Tell about a time when you used _____.

OR,

Draw or find a picture of how you *could* use this literacy action in your life.

HOW DID LITERACY BECOME LIBERATED?

The preceding true accounts were premised on the enduring story of literacy change. From the stone age to the digital age, literacy has experienced dynamic shifts. The segment that follows provides a description of these shifts and rationale for the attention literacy is receiving.

Why is literacy receiving attention unequaled to other 21st-century skills? Why does literacy symbolize security, freedom, creativity, and "the American way?" Is it the desire and will of our citizenry to provide a world-class education for each and every student enrolled in public, private, religious, and charter schools across the fifty states and territories that constitute the United States of America? How does literacy leadership transform practice and support the role educated citizens must assume in the 21st century? What questions have been silenced under the cloak of comprehension? Twenty years of formative and summative assessments administered by local, state, and federal groups collected data on fragmented task proficiency. Why? Consider one of the definitions for literacy used to shape instructional decisions: "The *chief* function of literacy is to make us *masters* of the standard instrument of knowledge and communication, *Standard Written English*, thereby enabling us to give and receive complex information orally and in writing over time and space" (Hirsch, 1988, p. 3).

The definition Hirsch provided in 1988 represented society's needs as they aligned with the literacy demands of the 20th century. Society's values and beliefs about literacy and learning expectations for every child are interlaced with economic connections fueling the race for global independence. Exhibit 1.9 takes a look at the progress of these connections and how they have iterated from the first markings on cave walls.

EXHIBIT 1.9

A Picture Walk of Literacy from the Stone Age to the Digital Age

1. 30,000 years ago—
Markings on cave walls conveyed meaning.

Reedin thse wrds mns U kn mak konections betwn mrks nd sondz

2. 5,000 years ago—
Systems of marks were used to capture sounds (phonemic awareness).

3. 450 B.C.—
Plato expressed concern that written language would minimize human memory.

4. 1450 A.D.—
With the invention of the printing press, for the first time lay people could access the Bible and other publications and begin controlling their own decisions and lives.

- Telegraph
- Telephone
- Movies
- Radio
- Television

5. 1850–1950—
The ways information was comprehended began to shift. The definition of literacy was influenced by spoken words.

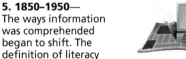

6. 1960s–1980s—
The development of Internet theory led to the creation of the Web. Learning was impacted as linear text was becoming unable to represent the connections among increasing amounts of information.

1998: Google
1999: Blogging
2001: iPod
2003: My Space; Second Life
2004: Facebook
2005: YouTube
2007: Kindle
2010: iPhone 4

7. 1998–2010—
In many cultures, a dozen years of immersion in technology expanded thinking and access to information. Cognitive dissonance increased between adolescents' capacity for information outside of school and the linear expectations inside of school.

8. Today,
we are no longer able to measure literacy progress by years. Literacy is not limited to a linear process. Rapid change is creating a literacy explosion.

Have you noticed how complexity of information, increased by technology, has intruded into traditional literacy expectations? Linear literacies grounded in society's demands from previous eras have gradually become insufficient to prepare intermediate and adolescent students in grades 4 through 12 to demonstrate connections between enormous amounts of information and knowledge that must be gleaned. The changing literacy demands of the 21st century begin in fourth grade and continue into high school (Carnegie Corporation, 2010, p. 1). The International Reading Association's literacy facts compiled in October 2008 by ProLiteracy Worldwide and Alliance for Excellent Education (www.proliteracy.org), listed below, support the urgent need to focus on literacy gaps:

- More than eight million U.S. students in grades 4–12 read below grade level. Most are able to sound out words, but cannot comprehend text.

- Annual health care costs in the United States are four times higher for individuals with low literacy skills than for individuals with high levels of literacy skills.

- American business spends more than $60 billion each year on employee training, much of that for remedial reading, writing, and mathematics.

- One-half of all adults in correctional institutions cannot read or write at all.

Society's needs have shaped expectations for learning. When Johannes Gutenberg made the Bible and other printed material available for all through his invention of the printing press, lay people were able to have more control over their personal lives and religious thought through independent reading. With this surge in literacy, the middle class experienced new opportunities for economic and societal participation. As iterations of literacy continued between1850 and 1950, is it not surprising that educators' expectations relied upon linear text-driven words, with students demonstrating knowledge graded for spelling, handwriting, and grammar? This remains true today. For example, during a Data Team meeting for collaborative scoring of comprehension responses, one teacher remarked that she always marks students down for spelling when using a comprehension rubric. When she asked if that was wrong, I responded with the question, "It depends on your purpose. If you want to determine instructional teaching points for comprehension, would spelling scores be helpful?" Reflection guided her response: "Maybe not."

When the Internet came into common use on personal computers, literacy was liberated. Complexity of knowledge connected with immediate global access, creating a gap between educators' perceived view of adolescent literacy and the realities of adolescent lives in the digital age.

TODAY'S CONTEXT FOR ADOLESCENT LITERACY

Intermediate and adolescent literacy includes the range of communication practices engaged in by students in grades 4 through 12. These practices extend beyond reading and writing, frequently referred to as "reading in the content areas," to speaking a heritage language at home, reading text messages from friends, and checking out multiple Web sites, all the while being expected to write traditional essays based on rubric indicators (Alvermann, 2009, p. 99).

A cornerstone of the current education reform movement, adolescent literacy achievement has been identified with laser focus by policy makers and administrators as an area requiring intense attention as a priority goal (Carnegie Corporation, 2010). And for good reason: while U.S. students' scores in grade 4 are among the world's best, our grade 10 students' scores are among the lowest. The No Child Left Behind Act's focus on "Reading First" for primary students had a positive impact, but was not an inoculation against adolescent failure. Strong readers and communicators are vital—they will provide our country with future scientists, engineers, and inventors. Therefore, "We need to ensure all states have strategic literacy plans for grades 4–12 ... and are working to ensure all schools have a way of embedding literacy into their designs" (Carnegie Corporation, 2010, p. 68).

THE DISCIPLINARY LITERACY FOCUS

Disciplinary Literacy instruction includes literacy connections within specific content areas. The focus of this instruction is to guide students to read specific content as an expert would. When students read texts while thinking as a historian, deeper understanding of that content is achievable. Our Disciplinary Literacy constructs and teaching models are based on the premise that "skills taught in English ... aren't sufficient to help students study math, science, history, or literature. Texts in these content areas have different structures, language conventions, vocabularies, and criteria for comprehension. Adolescents benefit from being let in on the secret" (Snow and Moje, 2010, p. 67). To support students and educators during these times of dynamic changes in literacy, it is necessary for us to take an honest look at the world our adolescent learners are living in to understand and connect with what motivates them and expand their patterns of thinking. We must be able to consider the increasing number of different types of literacy that exist.

THE DIFFERENT TYPES OF LITERACY

Over the years, a plethora of literacy types or categories have evolved. The abundance of literacy types has contributed to the confusion. The variety of literacy types can be attributed to the fact that expectations defining this term were posited by federal, state, and local governmental bodies, as well as business, community, and parental organizations. Such diversity of interest is necessary—to a point. Requiring education to address every nuance and responsibility has resulted in an overwhelming number of frames of reference for literacy, as represented in Exhibit1.10.

EXHIBIT 1.10   Types of Literacy for the 21st Century

Examples of Different Types of Literacy, Organized into Categories:

Content Literacy	Mathematical Literacy
Economic Literacy	Media Literacy
Financial Literacy	Multicultural Literacy
Functional/Basic Literacy	Numeracy Literacy
Global Awareness Literacy	Prose Literacy
Health Literacy	Quantitative Literacy
Information Literacy	Technological Literacy
Innovative Literacy	Visual Literacy

The historical lack of collective agreement throughout the United States about literacy standards and the fragmentation of expectations for students in preschool, elementary, middle, and high schools compounded the confusion. Expecting education to be responsible for *all* literacy types would seem like a perfect plot for a shocking new reality TV show, if it weren't already our current reality. Awareness of the different types of literacy enhances our understanding about the scope of literacy.

THE DEFINITIONS OF LITERACY FOR THE 21ST CENTURY

Before proceeding further, we must tackle the definition of literacy. Why are we not quoting a few definitions from the literature and moving on? Just as quick directions do not always provide the best route, definitions do not guarantee clarity.

Reeves highlighted the need for clarity about literacy when he said, "the progress of the past decade in research on literacy has little effect if leaders resort to simply repeating slogans and purchasing programs. Educational *leaders* believe that literacy is a priority, so they have a personal responsibility to be able to understand literacy instruction, to define it for their colleagues, and to observe it on a daily basis" (Reeves, 2009, p. 120). In support of Reeves' urgent demand, Chapter 3 details the Disciplined Practice literacy leadership model that directly connects leadership with literacy. It is our experience that leaders and learners recognize the need to understand literacy, but experience frustration due to its changing nature. Wherever we go, we are asked, "What is the definition of literacy?" The frequency of this question is identifying a priority need for understanding literacy with its range of skills, strategies, and processes.

Defining literacy to achieve clarity about meaning and its current relevance is necessary, but it requires reflective thinking, beyond clicking on a Wikipedia entry. Literacy definitions, when compiled over two decades, provide a picture of literacy's evolving character. The chronologically listed definitions in Exhibit 1.11 represent sources respected in the field of literacy. As a baseline, the traditional definition of literacy is considered to be the ability to read, write, listen, and speak.

Each literacy definition provides qualities that shape its meaning. Can acknowledging several definitions be confusing? Absolutely. *Shifting from decades of certainty framed by confident linear models to the present complexity surrounding literacy requires clear direction for instruction and leadership that acknowledges the dynamic nature of literacy and is accepting of evolving understanding.* We are offering a snapshot of current reality as a definition to provide clear direction that is capable of guiding leaders and learners directly into the heart of the literacy explosion to feel its pulse and grab hold of its potential.

Literacy's dynamic interactions empower disciplines, create understanding, and communicate knowledge, resulting in individual and societal transformation.

As you proceed further inside literacy, Chapter 2 will provide instructional connections, while Chapter 3 will establish connections with leadership. Chapter 4 will highlight support for struggling students and provide suggestions for sustainability.

EXHIBIT 1.11 **Literacy Definitions**

1988—Hirsch, p. 3—"The *chief* function of literacy is to make us *masters* of the standard instrument of knowledge and communication, *Standard Written English,* thereby enabling us to give and receive complex information orally and in writing over time and space."

2001—Webster's Online Dictionary—"The ability to read and write."

Webster's Online Dictionary provided the above as the definition in 2010, but stated it was from 2001. Comparing this definition with today's explosion of literacy reflects how our concept of literacy is changing. It appears that definitions may provide a progress-monitoring lens for literacy.

2005b—Gregory and Kuzmich, p. 7—"Literacy has four competencies: 1. Functional Literacy: Learning to read, write, speak, and listen 2. Content Literacy: Reading, writing, speaking, and listening to demonstrate content-area learning. 3. Technical Literacy: Using reading, writing, speaking, and listening in multimedia venues to create products and demonstrations of learning. 4. Innovative Literacy: Reading, writing, speaking, and listening to do or solve something complex, invent something unique, or produce something innovative."

*Notice how this definition embedded **types** of literacy within it to demonstrate connections and increasing complexity. As literacy evolved, it incorporated actions such as creating, solving, inventing, and producing.*

2008—National Council of Teachers of English Position Statement—"A collection of cultural and communicative practices shared among members of particular groups. As society and ethnology changes, so does literacy. Because technology has increased the intensity and complexity of literacy environments, the 21st century demands a literate person possess a wide range of abilities and competencies—many literacies. These literacies—from reading online newspapers to participating in virtual classrooms—are multiple, dynamic, and malleable."

2008—Coiro, Knobel, Lankshear, and Leu, pp. 23–24—"A rapid and continuous process of *change* in the ways in which we read, write, view, listen, compose, and communicate information. It may be that literacy acquisition is defined not by acquiring the ability to take advantage of the literacy potential inherent in any single, static technology of literacy, such as traditional print technology, but rather by a larger subset and the ability to continuously adapt to the new literacies required by the new technologies that rapidly and continuously spread on the Internet. Literacy will also include knowing how and when to make *wise decisions* about which technologies, and which forms and functions of literacy most support one's purposes."

It is interesting to note how acknowledgment of the pace of change, its causal impact on literacy, and interconnectedness with technology are finding their way into literacy definitions.

EXHIBIT 1.11   **Literacy Definitions** *(continued)*

2008—Gardner, p. 161—"The first cognitive assignment for all schools is mastery of the basic literacies of reading, writing, and calculation. Once one has become literate, by the end of the elementary years, the time is at hand for the acquisition of the major scholarly ways of thinking—at a minimum, scientific, mathematical, historical, and artistic.

2008—Shanahan and Shanahan, p. 6—"Literacy includes a base of generalizable basic skills, including decoding skills, understanding of various print and literacy conventions, etc. Most children master these kinds of skills and conventions during the primary grades. Most American students gain control of intermediate reading tools, such as comprehension strategies, by the end of middle school. In middle and high school, many students begin to master even more specialized reading routines and language, but these are constrained to most reading tasks. High school students' literacy needs to include proficiency with advanced, less generalizable skills embedded in disciplinary literacy."

2009—Hyerle, pp. 10–11—"21st-century literacy is visual-spatial-verbal-auditory. It can be represented in linear and non-linear forms."

2009—Hoffman and Goodman, pp. 98–99—"Adolescent literacy in 2009 refers to a vast array of reading, writing, and communicative practices in which young people engage."

2010—Jacobs, p. 102—"Global Literacy—We do not yet have an established nomenclature for the dimensions of the newly emerging field of global literacy, but it is generally agreed to include these elements: Skills to communicate in languages other than English, to work in cross-cultural teams, to assess information from different sources around the world . . ."
  p. 140—"Information Literacy—Searching for and locating accurate, reliable information on the Internet."
  p. 141—"Media Literacy—Education that aims to increase the students' understanding and enjoyment of how the media work, how they produce meaning, how they are organized, and how they construct reality."

2010—Carnegie Corporation, p. 10—"Specific combination of texts, content, and the many learning tasks to be performed at any given grade level—change and intensify quickly after fourth grade. Secondary students must also be able to interpret, critique, and summarize. Literacy skills and content knowledge are embedded in tasks and often invisible."

2011—Piercy and Piercy, p. 66—"Literacy's dynamic interactions empower disciplines, create understanding, and communicate knowledge, resulting in individual and societal transformation."

Disciplinary Literacy, as it honors specific and unique demands of the reader, and ways of thinking in different contents, is becoming evident in literacy definitions. While Disciplinary Literacy constructs are intentionally less generalizable across content areas than "reading in the content area" strategies, the literacy actions (Chapter 1) and Habits of Mind (Chapter 4) used in conjunction with the Disciplinary Literacy model do transfer to all contents, K–16 levels, and leadership. As time has passed, literacy definitions have expanded to purposefully reflect life changes. As a result, the definition of literacy will continue to evolve.

Literacy has journeyed from the concept of *mastery* in 1987 to *exploring* today. What lies ahead? As we have discussed, exploring shifting priorities in uncertain times will determine specific literacy needs to guide the future of instruction.

WHY IS LITERACY UNDER THE URGENCY SPOTLIGHT?

The pace of change during the first decade of the 21st century altered traditional understanding of reading comprehension. Today, isolated reading comprehension skills are blending into a Web-hosted database with access to unlimited data points and suggested literacy processes, practices, interventions, and models. The Carnegie Corporation (2010) recommends that state standards in all subject areas should make explicit the challenges of reading and writing within each discipline. This is supported by the Partnership for 21st Century Skills (2009), demonstrating how 21st-century skills can be integrated into the core subjects. Also, the Common Core State Standards Initiative for K–12 English Language Arts (2010) includes a companion document, "Standards for Literacy in History and Science 6–12" explicitly requiring "shared responsibility for literacy." No longer can instruction of reading, writing, and speaking be disaggregated and segregated to one specific curricular area or identified as the responsibility of a sole source provider of specific content knowledge.

Literacy is under the urgency spotlight; school and system leaders are accountable for providing clarity and direction. One component of literacy, reading tasks, had become the focus of heavily controlled state standards and federal regulations that molded reading to fit external expectations. Predetermined, specific, scientifically based reading researched strategies published by the National Reading Panel (2000) were to produce efficient Annual Yearly Progress (AYP) results. Questions have been controlled by prescribed, restricted expectations. As reading adapts to numerous cultures, migrates between populations, and resides on multimedia platforms, it merges with the richly blended components of literacy. In short, world changes outside of school are raising expectations inside of school. However, as Reeves (2009, p. 16) explains, instructional leadership "does not mean very much if the leaders and teachers hold vague and inconsistent views of the most essential elements of effective instruction in literacy." What begs to be asked needs to extend beyond reading comprehension performance on assessments to indicators of success as evidenced in learners and leaders *understanding, applying,* and *exploring* literacy actions to address the needs of their complex 21st-century lives. The urgent questions that must be asked to improve today's students' comprehension needs include:

1. To increase student capacity (compared to proficiency) to understand and apply (compared to just answer) the evolving (compared to fixed, scientifically-based,

previously identified) complexities of literacy (compared to isolated skills) throughout students' 21st-century lives, how can literacy be taught for understanding? (Chapters 1, 2, and 4)

2. What core literacy actions and Habits of Mind are vital for literacy development? (Chapters 1, 2, and 4)

3. What Disciplined Practice components provide leadership that supports urgent demands for increased literacy capacity while closing gaps in urban schools? (Chapter 3)

4. How can instruction honor the unique Disciplinary Literacy demands of specific content? (Chapter 2)

Notice how these questions build on current expectations while expanding connections. Data Teams, questions asked by leaders during Compelling Conversations with teachers, and the questions that are generated from these conversations have a profound impact on teachers' decisions and their students' learning.

A juncture in educational direction exists once again. Are we prepared to acknowledge the approaching literacy crisis stemming from the need to educate students in two languages—those of the pre- and post-digital worlds? Do educators require additional laws enacted by noneducators to resolve the increasing gap between students' 21st-century literacy needs and leadership practices? If not, let's step on the gas.

Chapter 1 Conclusion

Dear Readers,

From when today's adolescents first started school with their pencil cases and paper notebooks, the world of literacy has dramatically changed. Likewise, critical thinking needs have expanded to include flexibility in solving complex 21st-century problems. Literacy actions connect sets of different thinking processes with disciplines and life, enabling adolescents to intentionally and naturally draw upon specific thinking as needed, just as they select specific applications on their cell phones to achieve particular outcomes.

This chapter identified the foundations of Disciplinary Literacy and provided connections for learners, leaders, and adolescent citizen journalists. The next chapter establishes connections between the literacy actions in five disciplines using the Disciplinary Literacy investigation model. As the life-skills scenarios from this chapter depict, students need the strength of our united literacy beliefs to guide their learning and lives.

With appreciation for the past and anticipation of the future,

Thommie

CHAPTER 2

What Are the Disciplinary Literacy Instructional Models?

Literacy actions, as described in Chapter 1, are filters, used flexibly for *understanding, exploring*, and *sharing* our world. How does the concept of a filter change from one area of our lives to another? In short, how does the implied metaphor of filtering in the real world enhance our notion of what we believe our students must know and be able to do cognitively as stated in the Common Core State Standards? How can the Disciplinary Literacy model provided in this text specifically provide explicit, aligned instructional support for the fewer, clearer, higher expectations delineated in the "Common Core State Standards for English Language Arts & Literacy in History/Social Studies, Science, & Technical Subjects"?

Filters are a necessary part of our lives. We use them, replace them, and take them for granted. Oil filters, air filters, coffee filters. When I bought my first house, I quickly discovered a filter that I had never heard about or needed previously until discovering the unpleasant realities of "hard water." (If you have ever had hard water, you may know where I'm going with this analogy.) Water is considered hard if it contains a certain level of dissolved minerals, like iron, calcium, and others. Now this may sound benign, even healthy, but the presence of these minerals in a household water supply can lead to many inconveniences. I unintentionally created my first water "filter" when I spilled a glass of water on the dining-room carpet. Days later, despite my efforts to wipe it up, the spill spot on the carpet felt like sandpaper. As the water dried, the minerals were left crystallized on the carpet. The alarming image of "fossilized" carpeting in the entire house shot through my brain. It was then that a neighbor let me know about the local water and my need for a water filtration system—a softener. Basically, the filter in the softener traps the minerals, and flushes them out before they ever reach the faucets in our house, avoiding a whole host of problems (including carpet rough enough to be mistaken for a sidewalk in the dark).

Filters improve our lives. But the purposes and functions of filters extend far beyond our everyday experience with them. In fact, all of the branches of academia have differing understandings of what filters are and what they do. For example, in chemistry, a filter is basically a device, usually a membrane or layer, which is designed to physically block certain objects or substances while letting others pass. But if filters basically just block or minimize undesirable things, how will understanding them shed light on how we want our students to process the overwhelming amount of information that confronts them every day? Are there filters that do more? Does the analogy end here? Well, the world of computer programming views a filter in a more complete way. To programmers, a filter is a program that accepts a certain type of data as input, transforms it in some manner, and then outputs the transformed data. Here we have more at work than blocking; we have transforming. And we have always wanted our students to input knowledge, transform it in different ways, and produce evidence of that transformation that reflects learning. What types of filters would students need to read for true understanding? How would these filters change as the student moved from reading a history textbook chapter on the American Civil War to a science article on global warming? Before we begin to address these important questions, we should take a moment to understand current thinking about adolescent reading.

WHAT IS DISCIPLINARY LITERACY?

As described in Chapter 1, efforts to promote "reading in the content areas" have been less successful than expected; we have gradually come to realize that reading is not an add-on which can be universally applied to any content. Strategies and skills that were once thought to be a cure-all for poor comprehension have produced diminishing results. Recently, educational scholars have been asking if the academic contents themselves place specialized demands on readers beyond the scope of typical content-area reading instruction. The groundbreaking work of Dr. Tim Shanahan has addressed the specialized nature of content reading at the secondary level. Shanahan and Shanahan's research into literacy has reclassified the world of reading instruction into hierarchical categories depicted by a triangle having three segments. They define them as follows: **Basic Literacy**—"Literacy Skills such as decoding and knowledge of high-frequency words that underlie virtually all reading tasks" is located on the bottom third of the triangle; **Intermediate Literacy**—"Literacy skills common to many tasks, including generic comprehension strategies, common word meanings, and basic fluency" is represented in the middle of the triangle; and a new category, **Disciplinary Literacy**—"Literacy skills specialized to history, science, mathematics, literature, or some other subject" is represented by the top triangle segment (2008, p. 44). Significantly, the Intermediate Literacy phase, which most closely matches the typical secondary notion of "reading in the content areas," should end around the fifth grade, according to Shanahan and Shanahan's research. This means that for the average student, Disciplinary Literacy instruction should begin in earnest at the middle level and continue through high school. However, students in grades 4–12 are included in the changing literacy demands (Carnegie Corporation, 2010). These research-based insights have left the adolescent reading community with an instructional conundrum: How can we best equip students to navigate content-area text in a systematic manner that will promote literacy while capitalizing on the unique nature of the different content areas. Where is the confluence between content-specific reading demands and student capacity to flexibly apply filters to understand and extend meaning in text? Specifically, what instructional approach will enable our students to filter their reading for specific data using literacy actions, including *synthesizing* and *creating,* to cognitively transform learning? What would be necessary for a student to read a history text, or any text, as a historian would—filtering the words and sentences through questioning from the perspective of a historian, and transforming them into an understanding worthy of a historian? How about a scientist, mathematician, literary critic, or musician?

WHAT IS DISCIPLINARY LITERACY'S NEW MODEL FOR ADOLESCENT UNDERSTANDING?

We believe that the above is possible, even practical. To do so involves the synthesis of three elements: first, understanding why each of these disciplines is foundational to literacy; second, uncovering how the specific perspectives of practitioners in each of these areas informs their understanding of text; and finally, and most importantly, exploring how the four-stage investigation of text may be applied to different disciplines. Each discipline has correlating, print-ready student guide sheets. Each student guide sheet includes a question to stimulate critical thinking for at-risk students and/or English Language Learners (ELL), which has been differentiated for vocabulary as indicated by bold print. This chapter will describe the four-stage text investigation components of context, text, and two subtexts as they are applied in the disciplines of history, literature, science, math, and music, respectively. These instructional materials, designed specifically to generate deeper understanding in each of the disciplines listed above, may be used with standard curricular materials. We have found incorporating authentic texts, such as those available on the National Public Radio's feature "This I Believe" Web site (http://thisibelieve.org/essay/), expands opportunities for students to comprehend complex texts that support the Common Core State Standards expectations, state level curricula documents, and district curricula. Documents similar to those available on Web sites such as This I Believe, Our Documents.gov (http://www.ourdocuments.gov/), USA.gov (www.USA.gov/Topics/Reference_Shelf/Documents.shtml), and the Library of Congress Digital Collections (http://www.loc.gov/library/libarch-digital.html) provide experiences with comprehending texts that adolescents will encounter outside of school, during college, and throughout their careers and personal lives. A sample instructional, print-ready model for reading like a historian, using the primary document from This I Believe, "Free Minds and Hearts at Work" by Jackie Robinson, 1952, is included at the end of the Reading Like a Historian section in this chapter.

READING LIKE A HISTORIAN

To read like a historian, we must cultivate a working understanding of several things: Why does history matter? What do historians seek to know? How does their unique way of knowing inform an understanding of our world, others, and ourselves? And finally, how might we enable our students to apply literacy actions with the history filters to read like a historian?

Why Does History Matter?

Spending years within the walls of history classrooms has left many of us with an in-depth knowledge of specific areas of history. But how many of us, if asked why history, as a content area, matters in life, would be able to cobble together a meaningful answer? History teachers, of course, may have such responses at their fingertips, but maybe not. It seems that at the secondary level, we have suffered from content-driven nearsightedness. We focus on the information and instruction close at hand, the business of learning history, or math, or science, and neglect the response to the larger question of why history will or should matter to us. And if we, as educators, struggle to answer this basic question, how would our students respond? We must pause to remind ourselves, or realize for the first time, some of the reasons that we were required to spend all that time in history classes. We will briefly examine three justifications for the study of each discipline:

- **Civics**—How is history fundamental to citizenship?
- **Aesthetics**—How does history satisfy the human predilection for artistic appreciation?
- **Intellectual connectedness**—How does history connect to the other major areas of academic pursuit?

Civics—How is history fundamental to citizenship?

History opens the window to the vast amount that may be learned about human advancement. The lifespan of the average person, even if it were extended by a century, would leave relatively little time for learning through first-hand experience.

Now that may seem like a lot of time "to get our act together" on a personal level, but what would that teach us of the trials of being President of the United States, if we chose to be an accountant? History bridges the gap between the time we have to live and learn what it means to be a human and what can be known about the human experience during our lifetime. And what lessons history teaches us! By studying the past triumphs and tragedies of the human experience, we are released from the narrow confines of our own experiences. At its best, history enables us to analyze from a dispassionate distance the insights and errors of others, while vicariously reliving those events as they did. And when we apply the knowledge gleaned from historical study in combination with literacy actions, we are able to *infer* possible consequences, *apply* learnings from past errors, and *evaluate* the fault lines of our individual and collective lives by integrating these learnings when thinking and communicating as citizen journalists (see Chapter 1).

Aesthetics—How does history satisfy the human predilection for artistic appreciation?

Humans are capable of constructing the pyramids at Giza and the concentration camps of eastern Europe. The human race has been capable of great sacrifice and incredible selfishness. This poignant reality is both personal to us and general to our society, and it informs all aspects of our lives.

Intellectual Connectedness—How does history connect to the other major areas of academic pursuit?

History is the tapestry that records human innovation in science, tracks the evolution of mathematical awareness, and frames the context for the arts through time. It captures the great and small ideas and persons that have shaped the current of our society. In this sense, history is the living record of all the academic disciplines, if not the parent of them. Without at least a general understanding of the historical record, the true significance of every human achievement is obscured. Clearly, then, history as a discipline is worthy of focus in our students' instructional program and central to enabling them to understand, manage, and shape meaning in their world. But what is it that historians seek to know, and what truth do they strive to find?

> History is the living record of all the academic disciplines, if not the parent of them.

What Do Historians Seek to Know?

Woodrow Wilson clearly felt history's chief aim went beyond collecting names, dates, and summaries of important historical events; instead, the study of history was to develop in us "the invaluable mental power which we call judgment" (Wineburg, 2001, p. 5). In his seminal work on what it means to read like a historian, *Historical Thinking and Other Unnatural Acts*, Wineburg connects the study of history with knowing ourselves: "The familiar past entices us with the promise that we can locate our own place in the stream of time and solidify our identity in the present. By tying our own stories to those who have come before us, the past becomes a useful resource in our everyday life, an endless storehouse of raw materials to be shaped or bent to meet our present needs. Situating ourselves in time is a basic human need. Indeed it is impossible to conceptualize life on the planet without doing so" (2001, p. 7). But what are these "raw materials" that history provides? How might our students incorporate literacy actions to process them to meet present needs and develop sound interpretations that rise to the level of *judgments*?

Since our focus here is specifically on literacy, we must further question what historians look for in texts, the information they seek to filter, and how they use what they discover to inform the understanding that will lead to "mature historical thought." So what do historians do to build historical interpretations? Well, first, they view texts not as lifeless passages in a book, but as living "speech acts" (Wineburg, 2001, p. 66). A "speech act" is a communication (or a "text") that was produced by a specific person or persons, at a point in history (within a "context"), to fulfill a particular *purpose* or attain some *plan* (or an "impersonal subtext"), arising from various personal *motives* and *intentions* (or a "personal subtext"), which may have a significant impact on individuals and society. Here, then, is a model for reading like a historian through filtering

> **Speech Acts:**
> *Communication components: Context, Text, and two Subtexts*

texts. To build strong historical interpretations of text, students must incorporate *analyzing* for these four levels: context; text; and two subtexts: impersonal and personal. These components comprise our Four-Stage Model of Text Investigation, which we will explore for history, as well as literature, science, mathematics, and music.

Why do historians deliberately view acts of writing as *acts of speaking*? What is the benefit of consciously filtering text as though it were a speech or a conversation between the author and the reader? Well, when we engage in meaningful conversations, if we incorporate our Habits of Mind (Costa and Kallick, 2008) as described in Chapter 4, we not only listen to what is said to us, but we also "strive for accuracy" by *questioning*, confirming, or disagreeing. How we react to what is said usually changes based on the person we are speaking with, or the issue being discussed, or maybe even the events surrounding the conversation. In short, the *context* of what is said affects how we view the *text* of what is said, and most of us adapt our response naturally, either without much thought, or with much deliberate thought, depending on conditions. Often we listen between the words for what the speaker is really saying, or look behind the words for the reason they may be saying it. Here, we alert to the *subtext* of what is said: the speaker's motives and intentions, just as an adolescent's flowery compliments about how enjoyable dinner was may make us listen between and beneath the words for the request to use the family car, or to extend curfew.

How Can Reading Like a Historian Improve Adolescent Citizen Journalist Thinking?

Teaching students to deeply process the past precedes their ability to establish insightful connections with the present, which will enhance understanding about their changing future. With literacy evolving more rapidly, specific literacy actions establish connections among all disciplines by increasing capacity for synthesizing and developing patterns of meaning. Textbooks' limited perspective of the past is being replaced by unlimited digital access. How can adolescents make the most of enormous opportunities to thrive in their information-rich global society? Introduced in Chapter 1, the citizen journalist filter (Exhibit 1.4a) provides guiding questions to improve citizen journalist behaviors for adolescents in the following vital areas:

1. What questions do I need to ask myself to determine the *context* of the source of the information?

2. What questions do I need to ask myself when reading *unfiltered* information?

3. What questions do I need to ask *about* myself before preparing information for distribution?

When connected with "reading like a historian," students will be able to consider the basis of truth in a text, understand the message between the lines, and acquire deeper comprehension and insight about why the points were being made. Citizen journalists' responses require Habits of Mind, especially "thinking and communicating with clarity and precision," because adolescents must be honest with themselves about their own biases. They must be aware of their potential to have a positive global impact. Instruction to increase students' citizen journalist thinking is best begun with a real-life event, as in the high school dialogue below:

Citizen Journalist: Instructional Model

Teacher: I heard a car alarm in our school hallway yesterday and I didn't know what it was. How did I find out (and it was not from the administration)?

Student: You found out from us kids!

Teacher: Yes. Later today, you will be "thinking like a citizen journalist" as you are "reading like a historian."

Student: What is a citizen journalist?

Student: Someone who goes places and writes about what is happening.

Teacher: How do you learn as a citizen journalist?

Student: From other kids. From the Internet.

Teacher: Each of you is a citizen journalist, because I learned from you. How did you find out about what the noise was?

Student: Matt told me. He saw it.

Teacher: News went from one student to another. Today, so much news is straight from the source and each other. For example, yesterday when we heard an alarm I asked, "What is that? A car alarm in school?" I did not know. No adult sent me an e-mail. Then you guys walked into the class and told me someone broke the door to the defibrillator.

Student: Yes, because we were there when it happened. Then lots of people knew. I can send what I know to 200 people at one time. Then, they post to 500 Facebook friends, and they post to millions!

Teacher: You are citizen journalists. What is your responsibility to the people you are sending information to?

Student: To respond. To be truthful.

Teacher: People act on information. What if it is false? What is your responsibility *before* you send it to make sure it is true? This is important, because even in your adulthood, will you be reading filtered newspapers?

Students: "No!"

(The teacher distributes the Citizen Journalist Guide (Exhibit 1.4b) to help students reflect on their citizen journalist roles.)

The teacher summarized how "thinking like a citizen journalist" connects with "reading like a historian" because students need to know *motives*, just as in the news. When adolescents know the subtext behind an article, or even a text message, and possess deeper understanding about *why* the author made the point, they will be able to determine if it is true.

Disciplinary Literacy's Four-Stage Text Investigation: Reading Like a Historian

There is clear benefit, then, in viewing written texts as "speech acts." But this analogy does not account for the true complexity of understanding texts. We need a model that will enable us to break down the process of understanding into manageable components. So what are the stages of deep comprehension of text? First let's define them, before we explore how to provide a springboard for extensions beyond reading. And while these stages will remain the same for text in all disciplines, we will first examine them as they might be used by a historian, and by a nonhistorian who wants to be able to read like a historian.

> **Disciplinary Literacy's Four-Stage Model:**
>
> **A. Context**
> B. Text
> C. Subtext—Impersonal
> D. Subtext—Personal

Context—Stage A

Our word "context" derives from the Latin term *contextere*, which means "to join together." In a real sense, when we consider the background of something, we are piecing together clues that will help us to build the frame or larger picture that surrounds the thing we are considering. It is valuable to know that Lincoln's Gettysburg Address was given during a critical phase of the Civil War, even more so that it was given at the dedication of the cemetery for fallen soldiers after arguably the most critical battle of that war. When we reconnect text with its origins, details that might not strike the reader from a simple reading can become illuminated. As part of reading like a historian, reconstructing the context through incorporating literacy actions such as *questioning* and *applying* provides the raw materials needed for generating the investigation at the text and subtext levels. The Context Frame (Exhibit 2.1, Stage A) becomes a frame for answering the four questions. In each activity, differentiation for vocabulary is built into the activity by including questions designated in bold.

> **Disciplinary Literacy's Four-Stage Model:**
>
> A. Context
> **B. Text**
> C. Subtext—Impersonal
> D. Subtext—Personal

Text—Stage B

Our word "text" has a Latin root similar to that of "context": it is *textere*, which means "to weave together." Writers "weave" their thoughts and intentions for writ-

EXHIBIT 2.1 **Context Frame: History**

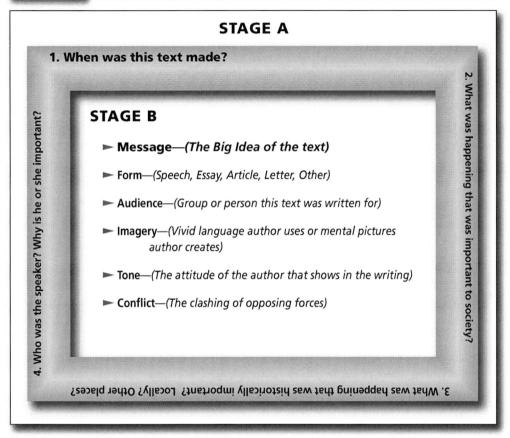

STAGE A

1. When was this text made?

2. What was happening that was important to society?

STAGE B

► **Message**—*(The Big Idea of the text)*

► **Form**—*(Speech, Essay, Article, Letter, Other)*

► **Audience**—*(Group or person this text was written for)*

► **Imagery**—*(Vivid language author uses or mental pictures author creates)*

► **Tone**—*(The attitude of the author that shows in the writing)*

► **Conflict**—*(The clashing of opposing forces)*

4. Who was the speaker? Why is he or she important?

3. What was happening that was historically important? Locally? Other places?

ing with the words, phrases, and sentences of their choosing to produce the fabric of their communication to the reader. Text questions include, "What is the author's message?" The answer to this question involves much more than we might think. The message of the text is driven by the ways the author chooses to communicate. And determining the message involves the literacy action of questioning and understanding key elements of the text. What form did the writer choose to carry the message? Who is the intended audience? What imagery has been included to spark the reader's imagination and transmit the subtleties of the author's ideas? And finally, what is the author's tone—the attitude he or she reveals through the writing? All of these elements are woven together to achieve the message, or the Big Idea, and must be analyzed together to understand the conflict (Exhibit 2.1, Stage B). Often, the most compelling aspect of any text is what the author doesn't directly reveal to us. All too frequently, however, readers end their journey for understanding once they grasp what's written on the page, unaware of a deeper meaning beneath the surface. Once the information surrounding the writing of the text is established by examining the context, and the text itself has been analyzed to establish its message, we must look beneath the surface of what has been said. This is the subtext.

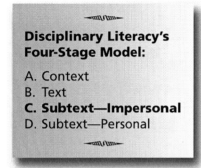

Disciplinary Literacy's Four-Stage Model:

A. Context
B. Text
C. Subtext—Impersonal
D. Subtext—Personal

Impersonal Subtext—Stage C

It is in the subtext that we must read between the lines to uncover the author's purpose and plan for writing and behind the lines to uncover the author's motives and intentions. To achieve this type of close reading—between and behind the lines—we must look at two areas of the subtext, the impersonal and the personal.

The first stage of subtext for us to consider is the impersonal subtext. This is where

EXHIBIT 2.2   **Reading Like a Historian Subtext Guide**

Stage C—Plan (a method for achieving an end)
What does the author plan to do or gain? What larger plan might the author have? Could it work? Why?

Stage C—Purpose (something set up and an end to be obtained)
What purpose did the author have in writing this text? Was it achieved?

Stage D—Intention (a decision to act a certain way)
What author's intentions can you uncover by reading between the lines of the text?

Stage D—Motive (a need or desire that causes a person to act)
What drove the author to write this text?

the reader's literacy actions of *inferring* and *evaluating* get a workout as the reader uncovers the unstated messages within a text by reading between the lines for the implications beyond the written word using the Subtext Guide (Exhibit 2.2, Stage C).

Sometimes these messages are subtle, sometimes not, as when Jackie Robinson, the first African-American to integrate into Major League Baseball, received an anonymous telegraph before a game in Cincinnati. The first part read: "Note. We have already got rid of several like you. One was found in a river" (Grunwald and Adler, 1999, p. 371). The anonymous authors didn't overtly threaten to murder Jackie, but it's hard to miss their meaning. Clearly, through this message, they planned to keep Jackie from playing in this game and likely other African-Americans from participating in the Major Leagues. And it's a short trip from this plan to their purpose: intimidation. This stage of investigation requires inferring the plan and purpose of the author, through the unraveling of the author's chosen words and phrases to reveal the meaning that lies between and behind the lines of the text. This Stage C is called "impersonal," because here, the reader deduces the plan and purpose of the author based on support from the context and text, while trying to maintain a personally neutral stance. The telegram Robinson received may shock or upset us, but the personal feelings we have should not get in the way of establishing the purpose and plan of the racist authors of the text.

Personal Subtext—Stage D

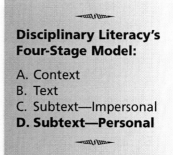

Disciplinary Literacy's Four-Stage Model:

A. Context
B. Text
C. Subtext—Impersonal
D. Subtext—Personal

At the deepest level of investigation of subtext, however, we sometimes uncover meanings which the author didn't intend to reveal, which have inadvertently become part of the fabric of the text. We might be reminded of the way in which scientists will often date an ancient garment by detecting the microscopic plant pollens trapped within its threads. These time-traveling bits of data weren't deliberately added, but they were infused when the garment was produced. At this stage, the reader becomes a type of archaeologist, *synthesizing*, *judging*, and reconstructing shards of meaning to reveal the motives and intentions of the author (Exhibit 2.2, Stage D). The motives beneath the writing may center on the author, revealing perspective or bias, or upon the reader, acting as a catalyst for altered personal views, enlightened understanding, or pointing toward issues which might impact society or warrant further investigation. But whatever the author's target, motive gives birth to intention, the desire to act. The components of the impersonal subtext—plan and purpose—and those of the personal subtext—intention and motive—form an interlocking scaffolding around the text. The definition of these terms in the Merriam-Webster Online Dictionary clearly demonstrates this relationship: the author's motive ("something—as a need or desire—that causes a person to act") gives birth to their intention ("a determination to act in a certain way"). Their intention, in turn, drives their purpose ("something set up as an object or end to be attained") which fuels the plan ("a method for achieving an end") of their writing. And while all four elements of subtext as presented in Exhibit 2.2—plan, purpose, intention, and motive—have a causal relationship, they need not necessarily always be addressed by students in that order.

To gear up literacy to reading like a historian, Exhibit 2.3 summarizes the moving parts that comprise the big picture of Disciplinary Literacy's Path of Action Gear for Reading Like a Historian.

While this method is quite different from what most students and teachers envision when they set about the task of comprehending a text, Wineburg reminds us it is much more natural than we may realize at first: "The comprehension of text reaches beyond words and phrases to embrace intention, motive, purpose, and plan—*the same set of concepts we use to decipher human action*" (Wineburg, 2001, p. 67). All of us expend mental energy trying to decipher why others—and even, we, ourselves— act in certain ways. Few of us, though, take the time to investigate the actions of others in the systematic way contained in the Four-Stage Model described above. Think of the power of our thinking if we would. Think of how our students would be empowered to comprehend text if they could frame the author's message through examining the context, could trace his or her specific purpose and detect the plan behind their writing, decipher the intention that instigated the author to write the text, and finally reconstruct the motive looming behind it all. And this depth could become the springboard for them to extend the act of understanding beyond the text, connecting it to themselves, and their quest for larger meanings as they communicate as citizen journalists. The student exemplars in Exhibit 2.4 are by at-risk adolescent readers in grade 9. The two exemplars, the Context Frame and the Subtext Guide, were generated following a "reading like a historian" lesson using the Associated Press story "Foiled Taliban Attack Using Boy, 14, Detailed" (Brummitt, 2010).

To guide adolescent citizen journalists' decisions, their thinking must be reflected upon. According to Hattie (2009, p. 22), "learning occurs when *learn* is the explicit goal" and when "there is deliberate practice aimed at attaining mastery of the goal." Visible learning occurs during Disciplinary Literacy instruction as students become passionate about the subject in reaction to questioning authors' motives, intentions, purposes, and plans. To support communication with integrity as citizen journalists, students respond to questions on the Personal Perspective Window (Exhibit 2.5) in any discipline.

EXHIBIT 2.3

Disciplinary Literacy's Path of Action Gear for "READING LIKE A HISTORIAN"

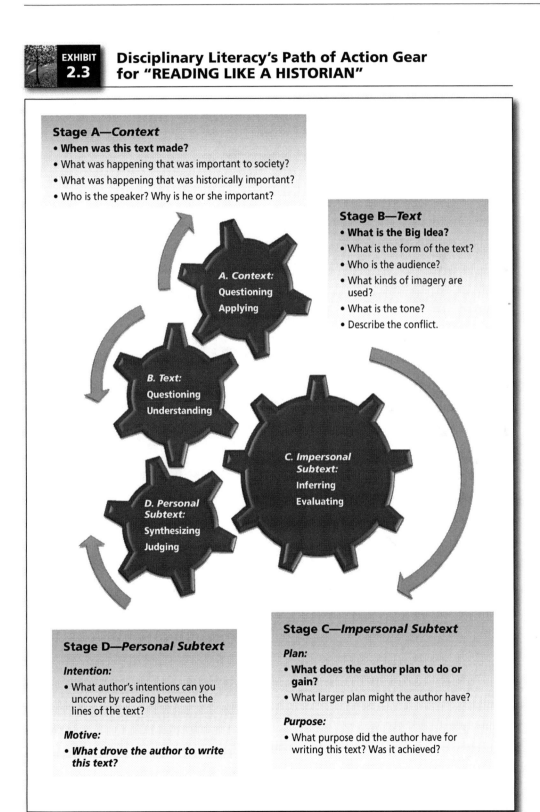

Stage A—*Context*

- **When was this text made?**
- What was happening that was important to society?
- What was happening that was historically important?
- Who is the speaker? Why is he or she important?

A. Context:
Questioning
Applying

Stage B—*Text*

- **What is the Big Idea?**
- What is the form of the text?
- Who is the audience?
- What kinds of imagery are used?
- What is the tone?
- Describe the conflict.

B. Text:
Questioning
Understanding

C. Impersonal
Subtext:
Inferring
Evaluating

D. Personal
Subtext:
Synthesizing
Judging

Stage D—*Personal Subtext*

Intention:

- What author's intentions can you uncover by reading between the lines of the text?

Motive:

- **What drove the author to write this text?**

Stage C—*Impersonal Subtext*

Plan:

- **What does the author plan to do or gain?**
- What larger plan might the author have?

Purpose:

- What purpose did the author have for writing this text? Was it achieved?

EXHIBIT 2.4 **Student Exemplars: Reading Like a Historian**

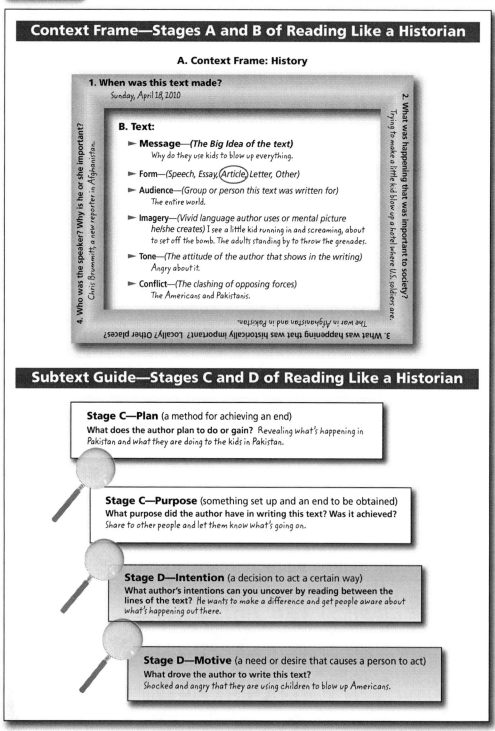

Context Frame—Stages A and B of Reading Like a Historian

A. Context Frame: History

1. When was this text made?
Sunday, April 18, 2010

2. What was happening that was important to society?
Trying to make a little kid blow up a hotel where U.S. soldiers are.

B. Text:

► **Message**—*(The Big Idea of the text)*
Why do they use kids to blow up everything.

► **Form**—*(Speech, Essay, (Article,) Letter, Other)*

► **Audience**—*(Group or person this text was written for)*
The entire world.

► **Imagery**—*(Vivid language author uses or mental picture he/she creates)* I see a little kid running in and screaming, about to set off the bomb. The adults standing by to throw the grenades.

► **Tone**—*(The attitude of the author that shows in the writing)*
Angry about it.

► **Conflict**—*(The clashing of opposing forces)*
The Americans and Pakistanis.

3. What was happening that was historically important? Locally? Other places?
The war in Afghanistan and in Pakistan.

4. Who was the speaker? Why is he or she important?
Chris Brummitt, a new reporter in Afghanistan.

Subtext Guide—Stages C and D of Reading Like a Historian

Stage C—Plan (a method for achieving an end)
What does the author plan to do or gain? Revealing what's happening in Pakistan and what they are doing to the kids in Pakistan.

Stage C—Purpose (something set up and an end to be obtained)
What purpose did the author have in writing this text? Was it achieved?
Share to other people and let them know what's going on.

Stage D—Intention (a decision to act a certain way)
What author's intentions can you uncover by reading between the lines of the text? He wants to make a difference and get people aware about what's happening out there.

Stage D—Motive (a need or desire that causes a person to act)
What drove the author to write this text?
Shocked and angry that they are using children to blow up Americans.

EXHIBIT 2.5 **Personal Perspective Window**

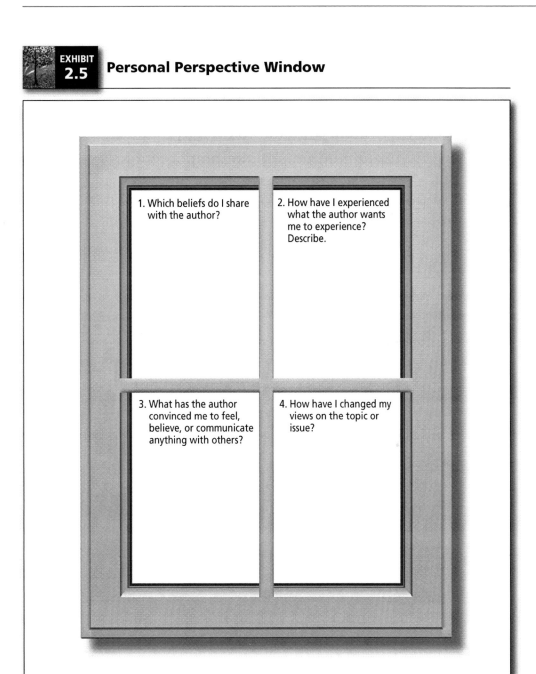

1. Which beliefs do I share with the author?

2. How have I experienced what the author wants me to experience? Describe.

3. What has the author convinced me to feel, believe, or communicate anything with others?

4. How have I changed my views on the topic or issue?

Extensions

1. My ongoing questions:

2. Ideas I want to explore and communicate:

The key is the engaging student dialogue as the teachers and students become learners. Disciplinary Literacy results in students becoming "self-determining" in their literacy lives and beyond (Pink, 2009, p. 71).

What Does Instruction for "Reading Like a Historian" Look Like?

So how does this 45-minute instructional model work in the classroom? The following brief segments demonstrate how grade 9 readers comprehend deeply while reading like a historian. Class 1 is a suburban high school, while Class 2 is an inner-city high school. Both classes are composed of challenged readers.

Class 1—Suburban High School—Reading Like a Historian—Grade 9 Challenged Readers

The text was an Associated Press online news story entitled "Foiled Taliban Attack Using Boy, 14, Detailed," published on April 18, 2010 (Brummitt). Students had two previous lessons using the Reading Like a Historian Disciplinary Literacy model. After briefly discussing the nature of the United States' struggle with the Taliban, the Context Frame for history was introduced (Exhibit 2.1). After students participated in reading the story aloud, they responded orally and in written form to the questions directly on the Context Frame: History guide sheet (Exhibit 2.1), before moving on to the second guide sheet, the Reading Like a Historian Subtext Guide (Exhibit 2.2). The snippets of dialogue below pick up after students completed their written responses on the Context Frame—Stage A. The teacher moves to Stage B to discuss the section on "imagery," defined as vivid language the author uses or mental pictures he or she creates.

> **Teacher:** Using the Context Frame, describe your imagery—as you were reading—in the center of the frame, in the Stage B section.
>
> **Student:** I see a little kid running. I see people hiding in bushes.
>
> **Student Written Response:** I see a little kid running in and screaming, about to set off the bomb. (I see) The adults standing by to throw the grenades.
>
> Following a discussion, the teacher moves on to "tone," defined as the attitude of the author that shows in the writing.
>
> **Teacher:** We should not be able to see the newspaper's attitude—only facts, not opinion.
>
> **Student:** That's bullcrap. Authors *do* give their opinion!

Student Written Response: Angry about it.

The teacher concludes the lively, engaged discussion of the Context Frame for context and text. She takes advantage of the natural opportunities, or teachable moments, such as delving into authors' opinions. Next, the teacher distributes the subtext guide sheet (Exhibit 2.2). After reviewing the guide sheet, the graphics on the guide sheet are discussed. The teacher moves on to Stage C, "plan," defined as a method for achieving an end.

Teacher: The magnifying glasses mean we are looking deeper. The author is revealing deeper what is happening in Pakistan and what they are doing to kids.

Student: In World War II, did they blow up kids?

Teacher: I do not think so, but our soldiers were young.

Student: I heard they had children hide under planes and blow them up. Why would they want to die?

Teacher: They have a different value of life. It is hard for us to understand.

Student Written Response: Stage C—Plan—Revealing what is happening to the war in Pakistan and what they are doing to the kids in Pakistan.

The teacher moves down to Stage D—"intention," defined as a decision to act in a certain way.

Teacher: What was the reporter's intention for writing?

Student: He thought it was a shocking deal and others should know. Reading between the lines, the author is scared. He is scared for the kids.

Student: I do not think he cares about the kids. He wants to make a difference and get more people in the army to help, by making us aware. If he really cared, he would do more for kids.

Student Written Response: Intention—He wants to make a difference and get people aware of what's happening out there.

As an extension activity, the teacher distributes a current newspaper to each student to read an article about the terrorist who attempted to explode a car bomb in New York's Times Square on May 1, 2010.

Student (who is holding a newspaper): How do you open this up?

Teacher: What is the connection between what we read and this article?

Student: This man could have been training with them.

Student: He could have been in New York in the same hotel preparing it. He is a U.S. citizen, although born in Pakistan.

Student: It would have happened again, like at the World Trade Center!

The dialogue depicts the capacity of challenged readers to think critically when engaged with relevant texts, including those having appropriate grade-level text complexity, as defined by the Common Core State Standards.

These lessons provide a two-way street for learning as teachers acquire insight about adolescents' perspectives—including their value of traditional newspapers!

Class 2—Inner-City High School—Reading Like A Historian

The text was George W. Bush's Address to Congress on September 20, 2001, available online. The segment began with, "Tonight, we are a country awakened to danger and called to defend freedom." This was the students' first attempt to use the "reading like a historian" model. After briefly discussing the context of the speech, the Context Frame for history was introduced (Exhibit 2.1). Students participated in reading the speech aloud, and responded using the Context Frame guide sheet. When students include misinformation in their dialogue, opportunities for instructional teaching points are provided, either during the dialogue or later in the class. The segment of the dialogue picks up with students discussing question number two on the Context Frame—Stage A:

Teacher: Turn the frame around to the next question—number two— What was happening at that time?

Student: I saw a movie—a documentary about Pakistan. While it—911— was happening, Bush didn't know what was happening. He was reading a book to little kids.

Student: In his speech, he was trying to send a message—like he was going to get him. He needed to know where to look for bin Laden.

The teacher refocused students on Stage B—Text, in the center of the frame.

Teacher: Imagery—What does "imagery" mean?

Student: You're imagining something. It's like when you read, you see it.

Teacher: Think for a minute about the passage you just read. What are you imagining is happening around you? What do you see that may not be in the text? Close your eyes.

Student: War.

Student: It was payback time; that is why we are in the war now.

Teacher: Can you share your thoughts further?

Student: Bush wasn't sincere. That's my opinion. In this speech, he was just trying to make people feel comfortable. And feel better about the situation.

The teacher directed students to the Reading Like a Historian Subtext Guide (Exhibit 2.2).

Teacher: Now I want you to please do one more thing. To practice reading like a historian, begin to think about what the author of this document tried to do to get you to understand what happened on September 11. Work with me. Are you willing to do that?

Teacher: Find "Stage C—Plan"—What does the author (President Bush) plan to do with this speech?

Student: Share his feelings about what was happening in America.

Teacher: Why did he write it? What was his purpose?

Student: To inform us about what was happening.

Student: He is helping the world by giving us facts. Fact is right.

Teacher: How would you feel if it wasn't fact?

Student: I cannot determine fact from my opinion. Is it my opinion? Because, in his speech on this handout, what Bush is saying looks different from the facts.

Teacher: How do you know if he is sincere about this speech? What is his motive?

Student: Body language.

Student: But we weren't there.

Student: He is not coming from his heart. Not just from this speech, but in other things he did. That is why he got kicked out of the house— The White House.

Following a clarifying discussion, the teacher proceeded.

Teacher: When you read, what happens to help you understand what you read?

Student: I think; I remember; you realize what you do not know. It all happens.

Student: I thought about suffering and families and made connections.

Teacher: Why do you remember so much about 9/11?

Student: It was my birthday! I was six.

Analyzing the responses from these two classroom extremes as classroom models from opposite ends of the "opportunity to learn" continuum based on poverty, culture, learning conditions, and family structure, provided several similar and interesting conclusions about using the Four-Stage Model for Text Investigation for reading like a historian. First, this approach to text comprehension, once students have become familiar with the use of the guide sheets, generates much motivation. Also, challenged students interact with text much more actively than is typical. The inner-city school was recently "zero-based"—every single adult was replaced as a result of poor student progress. Yet, potential and dynamic student engagement were apparent. And much of that interaction involved making personal or intellectual connections. Inaccurate connections expose misconceptions that can be addressed by the teacher directly or by further research. And finally, when students become fluent with the Four-Stage Model, its use is quick and efficient.

Instructional Model: Reading Like a Historian

This instructional, copy-ready model for reading like a historian, using a primary document from the This I Believe Web site (http://thisibelieve.org/essay/), "Free Minds and Hearts at Work"* by Jackie Robinson, provides immediately transferable lesson materials for Disciplinary Literacy instruction.

---

* "Free Minds and Hearts at Work" written by Jackie Robinson. From the book, *This I Believe*, edited by Jay Allison and Dan Gediman. Copyright © 2006 by This I Believe, Inc. Reprinted by arrangement with This I Believe, Inc.

"Free Minds and Hearts at Work"

By Jackie Robinson, 1952

At the beginning of the World Series of 1947, I experienced a completely new emotion when the National Anthem was played. This time, I thought, it is being played for me, as much as for anyone else. This is organized Major League baseball, and I am standing here with all the others; and everything that takes place includes me.

About a year later, I went to Atlanta, Georgia, to play in an exhibition game. On the field, for the first time in Atlanta, there were Negroes and whites. Other Negroes, besides me. And I thought: What I have always believed has come to be.

And what is it that I have always believed? First, that imperfections are human. But that wherever human beings were given room to breathe and time to think, those imperfections would disappear, no matter how slowly. I do not believe that we have found or even approached perfection. That is not necessarily in the scheme of human events. Handicaps, stumbling blocks, and prejudices—all of these are imperfect. Yet, they have to be reckoned with because they are in the scheme of human events.

Whatever obstacles I found made me fight all the harder. But it would have been impossible for me to fight at all, except that I was sustained by the personal and deep-rooted belief that my fight had a chance. It had a chance because it took place in a free society. Not once was I forced to face and fight an immovable object. Not once was the situation so cast-iron rigid that I had no chance at all. Free minds and human hearts were at work all around me; and so there was the probability of improvement. I look at my children now, and know that I must still prepare them to meet obstacles and prejudices.

But I can tell them, too, that they will never face some of these prejudices because other people have gone before them. And to myself I can say that, because progress is unalterable, many of today's dogmas will have vanished by the time they grow into adults. I can say to my children: There is a chance for you. No guarantee, but a chance.

And this chance has come to be, because there is nothing static with free people. There is no Middle Ages logic so strong that it can stop the human tide from flowing forward. I do not believe that every person, in every walk of life, can succeed in spite of any handicap. That would be perfection. But I do believe—and with every fiber in me—that what I was able to attain came to be because we put behind us (no matter how slowly) the dogmas of the past: to discover the truth of today; and perhaps find the greatness of tomorrow.

I believe in the human race. I believe in the warm heart. I believe in man's integrity. I believe in the goodness of a free society. And I believe that the society can remain good only as long as we are willing to fight for it—and to fight against whatever imperfections may exist.

My fight was against the barriers that kept Negroes out of baseball. This was the area where I found imperfection, and where I was best able to fight. And I fought because I knew it was not doomed to be a losing fight. It couldn't be a losing fight—not when it took place in a free society.

And; in the largest sense, I believe that what I did was done for me— that it was my faith in God that sustained me in my fight. And that what was done for me must and will be done for others.

⬥

In 1947, Jackie Robinson pioneered the integration of American professional athletics by becoming the first black player in Major League Baseball. During his 10 seasons with the Brooklyn Dodgers, he played on six World Series teams and was voted the National League's Most Valuable Player in 1949.

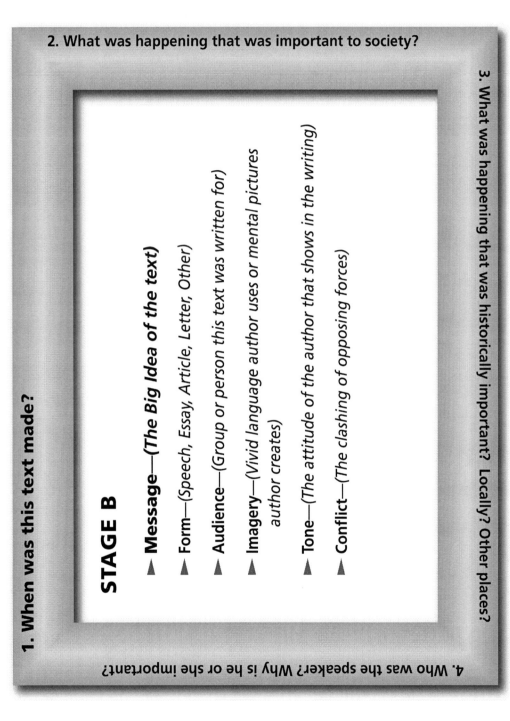

2. What was happening that was important to society?

STAGE A

1. When was this text made?

STAGE B

▲ **Message**—*(The Big Idea of the text)*

▲ Form—*(Speech, Essay, Article, Letter, Other)*

▲ Audience—*(Group or person this text was written for)*

▲ Imagery—*(Vivid language author uses or mental pictures author creates)*

▲ Tone—*(The attitude of the author that shows in the writing)*

▲ Conflict—*(The clashing of opposing forces)*

3. What was happening that was historically important? Locally? Other places?

4. Who was the speaker? Why is he or she important?

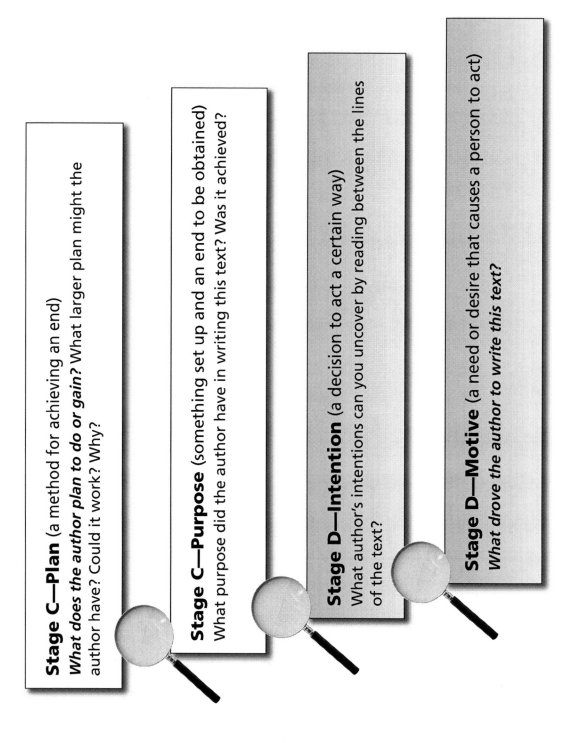

Stage C—Plan (a method for achieving an end)
What does the author plan to do or gain? What larger plan might the author have? Could it work? Why?

Stage C—Purpose (something set up and an end to be obtained)
What purpose did the author have in writing this text? Was it achieved?

Stage D—Intention (a decision to act a certain way)
What author's intentions can you uncover by reading between the lines of the text?

Stage D—Motive (a need or desire that causes a person to act)
What drove the author to write this text?

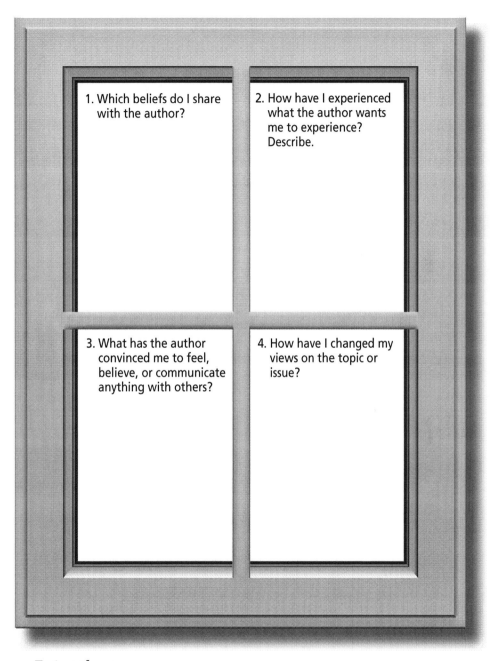

1. Which beliefs do I share with the author?

2. How have I experienced what the author wants me to experience? Describe.

3. What has the author convinced me to feel, believe, or communicate anything with others?

4. How have I changed my views on the topic or issue?

Extensions

1. My ongoing questions:

2. Ideas I want to explore and communicate:

READING LIKE A LITERARY CRITIC

We now turn our attention to another discipline area that secondary students spend much time studying: literature. While literacy skills certainly apply to the study of literature, our goal is to understand how literary critics engage with fiction to gain insight into what is gleaned from literature. How does reading like a literary critic using the Four-Stage Text Investigation Model support adolescents by providing them with the literary critic's unique way of knowing text? First, as we did with history, we must determine why the study of literature should matter to all of us. As before, we will look at the arguments from civics, aesthetics, and intellectual connectedness perspectives to determine why literature is a vital content focus for our students.

Why Does Literature Matter?

Civics

At its base, literature is about life. As individuals, we are all limited by time and space, by how much we can experience, and where we can experience it. Literature provides us with the opportunity to escape these limitations, to experience life vicariously through others, even if they are fictitious. Langer observes: "All literature—the stories we read as well as those we tell—provides us with a way to imagine human potential. In its best sense, literature is intellectually provocative as well as humanizing, allowing us to use various angles of vision to examine thoughts, beliefs, and actions" (1995, p. 5). Literature has always served to deepen our awareness of ourselves and others, promoting understanding, empathy, and tolerance—critical capacities for engaged citizens of all ages.

Aesthetics

One of the fundamental goals of any art form is to convey or arouse emotion. Unlike most other art forms, literature uses language as the vehicle for prompting an emotional reaction from the reader. The emotional experiences of literature connect reader and author, as well as reader and reader, and reader and society through shared vicarious experience. As a result, our self-awareness and ability to empathize with others expands.

Intellectual Connectedness

Literature carries the experience of human societies in a personal way, a way that history does not on its surface, a way that science and math, though they bind us through knowledge and discovery and potential, cannot. Noble Laureate Aleksandr Solzhenitsyn saw this role of literature as vital to any nation: "Literature conveys irrefutable condensed experience . . . from generation to generation. Thus it becomes the living memory of a nation. Thus it preserves and kindles within itself the flame of her spent history, in a form that is safe from defamation or slander. In this way, literature, together with language, protects the soul of a nation" (Solzhenitsyn, 1970, p. 5). Literature, then, has the power to weave the separate strands of human pursuit into a comprehensive fabric of human experience. Mathematical insight fuels our technological advancement. Science deepens our ability to advance human society. History forms the record of our collective and individual triumphs and failures. Music provides insight about connections between all disciplines and life. But only literature provides a universally appealing, personalizing framework capable of bringing these truths with emotional impact to the human soul.

What Do Literary Critics Seek to Know?

Clearly, the discipline of literature has much to offer society and each of us as individuals. But how is it relevant to our students, and how is it central for adolescents in their development as citizen journalists? To respond to this question, the following section provides an overview of the elements of literature as represented in Exhibit 2.6.

Langer sees that the study of literature empowers students: "Through literature, students learn to explore possibilities and consider options for themselves and humankind. They come to find themselves, imagine others, value difference, and search for justice. They gain connectedness and seek vision. They become the literate thinkers we need to shape the decisions of tomorrow" (1995, p. 1). The discipline of literature has always been acknowledged as having the potential to humanize students. It helps students develop Habits of Mind to expand their capacity to feel in order to enable them to develop the qualities that Langer identifies, qualities fundamental to understanding their world and growing as citizens.

What Are the Elements of Literature?

But what do serious students of literature seek to filter from texts? What is the *input* they seek? Which elements will promote literacy across different disciplines? Of the many concepts that students of literature filter text for, there are three that have the capacity to produce enriched understanding. They are the elements of *connection, empathy,* and *emotional truth.*

Connection

The first of these elements—connection—sets the stage for those that follow. The very nature of literary writing gives us a backstage pass to a character's life, a glimpse

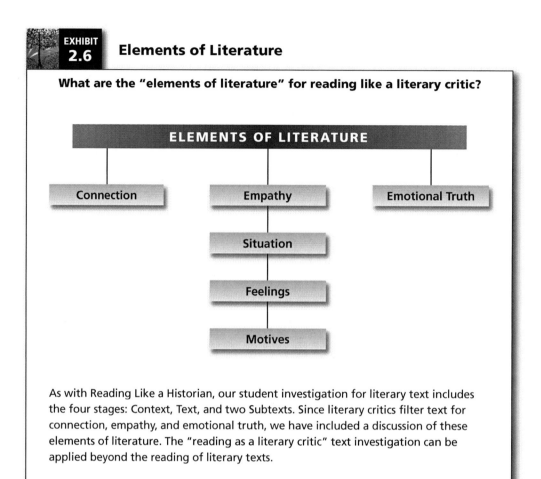

EXHIBIT 2.6 **Elements of Literature**

What are the "elements of literature" for reading like a literary critic?

ELEMENTS OF LITERATURE

Connection   Empathy   Emotional Truth

Situation

Feelings

Motives

As with Reading Like a Historian, our student investigation for literary text includes the four stages: Context, Text, and two Subtexts. Since literary critics filter text for connection, empathy, and emotional truth, we have included a discussion of these elements of literature. The "reading as a literary critic" text investigation can be applied beyond the reading of literary texts.

at those universal human emotions, thoughts, struggles, and experiences that have impacted our lives directly or indirectly. We move from the external differences between ourselves and the characters (race, gender, social status, nationality, etc.) into the internal realm of their thoughts, feelings, and motives. In short, we are granted the ability to see through their eyes, looking out on their world and, by extension, back on ourselves. This connectedness is possible because of the style of literature: we are drawn into a character's world and thoughts naturally during the very act of reading. *But what is designed to happen automatically within literature must be transferred to reading nonfiction texts, those texts students will encounter daily in the world, not just those that provide an imaginative escape from the world through narrative. In short, literate students must intentionally com-*

> Literate students must intentionally compare and contrast themselves with the author or a key person discussed in a nonfiction text.

pare and contrast themselves with the author or a key person discussed in a nonfiction text. "Key person" has been added as a target for student consideration due to, in part, the Informational Standards adolescents are expected to achieve in the English Language Arts Common Core State Standards, while also becoming responsible citizen journalists. To form connection, which is defined as an "association or relationship," students must ask themselves two related questions: "In what ways am I different from the author or key person?" and "In what ways am I similar to the author or key person?" Once differences have been successfully explored, the meaningful similarities may be successfully targeted: "Like Dr. King, I have struggled to make sure I treat all people with respect." And here, in the similarities, lies the possibility for making connections between the reader and author or the readers and key person presented in the text. These connections will set the stage for a deeper level of seeking enriched understanding of text.

Empathy

At this deeper level, the reader begins to open the door to the next crucial element of reading like a literary critic: empathy. Empathy has varying definitions, but the general consensus of these focuses on the ability to identify with and understand another's situation, feelings, and motives. Let's focus first on situation. The deliberate act of comparing and contrasting myself to an author or key person in a nonfiction text gives me the basis for understanding the real heart of where someone else is "coming from." That is, since I know how I, as a middle-aged male teacher in 2010, am similar to and different from Helen Keller, a 19th-century female leader, educator, and activist who was blind and deaf from birth, I can, therefore, begin to appreciate her situation—the conflicts and events in her life that ultimately shaped her beliefs. And beliefs are the key component for understanding someone's situation, the most accessible stage of empathy. Questioning what shaped another's beliefs provides a richer understanding of their situation in life. In literature, characters' beliefs are fueled in large part by the events of the plot, most especially by conflict. It is conflict that reveals character or shapes it. Therefore, reading like a literary critic for conflict in nonliterary texts should enable students to more fully understand another's situation, the first component of *empathy*. Most of us have never rushed into a burning building to save a stranger, but can we live the gut-wrenching turmoil of that action through the character of a firefighter? Can we experience the grief of the children left behind when the house explodes, and the spouse whose nights worrying have become a startling finality in an instant? How about the fire chief who ordered all personnel to stand down? In the case of conflict, what is true of fiction is true of life. Conflict has the power to deeply ingrain beliefs or alter them in an instant. By reading like a literary critic, students understand the relationship between conflict and belief and transform that relationship into empathy.

The next element in generating empathy within us as readers is to filter text for the feelings it contains. It is important to note that the feelings to be focused on here are those contained within the text, not the feelings aroused in the reader. (The latter will constitute the raw materials for the final element, emotional truth.) To understand the feelings encapsulated within the text, the reader must answer two questions. First, "What feelings does the author communicate in the text?" And next, "Why does the author share those feelings?" With the response to this second question, we have worked our way down to motive. As with reading like a historian, motive refers to a need or desire that causes a person to act. Yet, motive does not exist in isolation; it is interconnected with intention, purpose, and plan. When students reach this point in their filtering of text to read like literary critics, they have established connections to and built empathy toward the author or key person presented in the text.

Emotional Truth

The final task of the literary critic is transforming the above insights into *emotional truth*. In terms of reading like a literary critic, this is the "whole ball of wax" for our students. So what is this "emotional truth"? While history and literature both seek truth, as do science and mathematics, for that matter, literature has the capacity to elicit emotional truth within the reader. Spurgin has observed, "At its best, fiction leads us to thinking about feeling." Thinking about feeling involves two stages: First, identifying the emotional reaction aroused in us by the text, and then, "turning that reaction into the object of intellectual reflection." The end result of this intellectual reflection for the reader is the answer to the question "How has this (text) exposed me to myself?" (2009, Lecture 4).

Students seldom are directed to reflect in a meaningful way on feelings aroused from reading. If this does happen for students, it is most likely to occur in their study of literary text. How much more valuable would it be for adolescents to filter for and process their emotional reactions to texts about the Iraq war, global warming, gang violence, or world hunger? To arrive at emotional truths from text, to reach Spurgin's goal of understanding how a text can expose a reader to himself or herself, three questions must be answered: The first question, "What feelings did the text cause me to feel?" leads to the second question, "What do these feelings show me about myself?" Learning about obstacles overcome by Helen Keller may show a reader that what they consider insurmountable in life … isn't. As deep as these insights may be, they have not yet risen to the level of emotional truth. A final question remains: "What do I realize now because of these feelings that I didn't realize before?" An article about global warming may lead to feelings of fear for the earth's future, revealing to a reader that they have taken the natural world around them for granted. However, the resulting realization, the emotional truth, might be that taking things for granted can cause tragedy, in nature and maybe in relationships.

Teaching students how to filter nonliterary texts as literary critics is a tall order. The skill of reading like a literary critic is a vital part, or needs to be a vital part, of every student's academic achievement. While the process described above is not as clean or direct as the quadratic equation or the law of gravitation, its rewards are worthy of the effort. And now that we have an idea of what is to be gained from adopting the approach of the literary critic, we must focus briefly on how to do so. As with reading like a historian, we must see how the four stages for reading like a literary critic may be applied beyond the reading of literary text and generalized to other texts. We know that literary critics incorporate literacy actions such as *synthesizing* and *analyzing* to filter text for connection, empathy, and emotional truth, and we have reviewed the questions students must ask for each of these elements to develop enriched understanding of text. As with history before, and math and science to come, we will separate our student-based investigation of texts into a Four-Stage Model analysis of context, text, and subtext (both impersonal and personal).

Disciplinary Literacy's Four-Stage Text Investigation: Reading Like a Literary Critic

Context—Stage A

The Disciplinary Literacy model for reading like a literary critic guides explicit instruction for each component. As with history, our goal is for students to place the text within its original environment. However, here we begin with a focus on the author and message, rather than contemporaneous events surrounding the text and the author's connection to those events, using the Context Frame: Literature (Exhibit 2.7, Stage A).

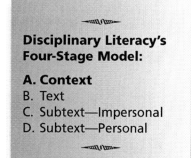

Disciplinary Literacy's Four-Stage Model:

A. Context
B. Text
C. Subtext—Impersonal
D. Subtext—Personal

Furthermore, prompting the reader to apply the literacy actions of connecting and questioning to determine the author's connection to the topic are the crucial raw materials which will enhance deep comprehension. While these elements of context will develop as the text and subtext are analyzed, they absolutely stimulate the thinking necessary for understanding the other aspects of the text.

EXHIBIT 2.7 **Context Frame: Literature**

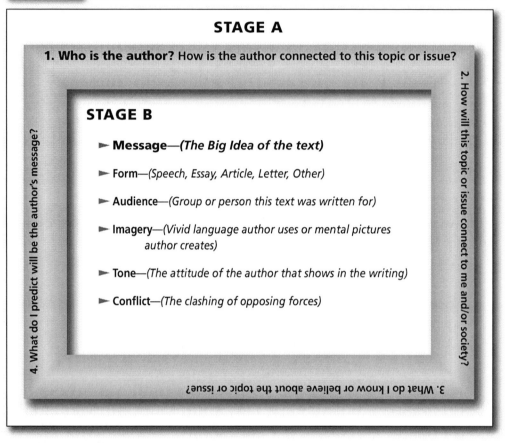

STAGE A

1. Who is the author? How is the author connected to this topic or issue?

4. What do I predict will be the author's message?

2. How will this topic or issue connect to me and/or society?

STAGE B

➤ **Message**—*(The Big Idea of the text)*

➤ **Form**—*(Speech, Essay, Article, Letter, Other)*

➤ **Audience**—*(Group or person this text was written for)*

➤ **Imagery**—*(Vivid language author uses or mental pictures author creates)*

➤ **Tone**—*(The attitude of the author that shows in the writing)*

➤ **Conflict**—*(The clashing of opposing forces)*

3. What do I know or believe about the topic or issue?

Disciplinary Literacy's Four-Stage Model:

A. Context
B. Text
C. Subtext—Impersonal
D. Subtext—Personal

Text—Stage B

The components of message, form, audience, imagery, tone, and conflict that form the analysis of the text for reading like a historian are the same here, as included on the Context Frame: Literature (Exhibit 2.7, Stage B). When reading like a literary critic, it is *understanding* the conflict that provides a connecting point for the growth of empathy.

Impersonal Subtext—Stage C

As when reading like a historian, the first level of subtext for us to consider is the impersonal subtext (Exhibit 2.8, Stage C).

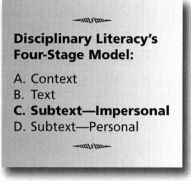

Disciplinary Literacy's Four-Stage Model:

A. Context
B. Text
C. Subtext—Impersonal
D. Subtext—Personal

At this level, our fundamental goal shifts from determining the author's purpose and plan, as we did for reading like a historian, to the literary critic's emphasis on connecting with the author or key person presented in a text. This is accomplished through personal comparison and contrast, along with analysis of the author's situation (the first stage of empathy). Identifying and understanding another's situation is achieved by *evaluating* the beliefs of the author or key person and *inferring* how conflict helped to shape those beliefs.

EXHIBIT 2.8 **Reading Like a Literary Critic Subtext Guide**

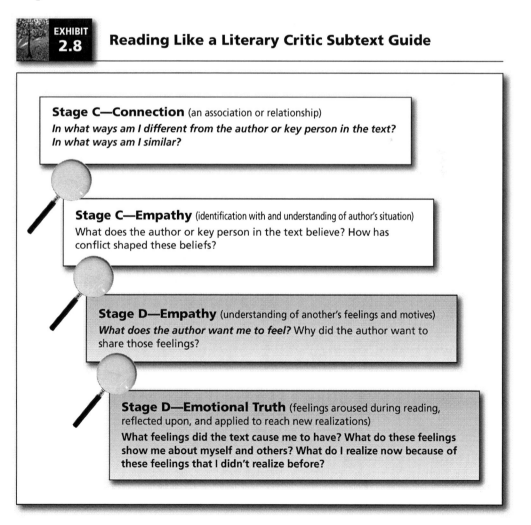

Stage C—Connection (an association or relationship)
In what ways am I different from the author or key person in the text? In what ways am I similar?

Stage C—Empathy (identification with and understanding of author's situation)
What does the author or key person in the text believe? How has conflict shaped these beliefs?

Stage D—Empathy (understanding of another's feelings and motives)
What does the author want me to feel? Why did the author want to share those feelings?

Stage D—Emotional Truth (feelings aroused during reading, reflected upon, and applied to reach new realizations)
What feelings did the text cause me to have? What do these feelings show me about myself and others? What do I realize now because of these feelings that I didn't realize before?

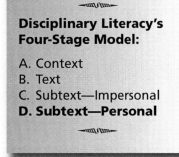

Disciplinary Literacy's Four-Stage Model:

A. Context
B. Text
C. Subtext—Impersonal
D. Subtext—Personal

Personal Subtext—Stage D

For the personal subtext, we shift from the reading like a historian goals of determining the author's intention and motive. For the literary critic, the personal subtext (Exhibit 2.8, Stage D) stage is focused on the remaining components of empathy—the feelings of the author and what the author wants me to feel, and motive—a need that causes action, filtered with the question, "Why did the author share those feelings?" requiring *synthesizing* and *judging*. This is followed by examination of the personal feelings aroused in the reader and transforming that reflection into emotional truth.

Finally, before we shift our focus to reading like a scientist, which should be refreshing in its lack of focus on emotion, we must admit that not every nonliterary text will prompt connections, stimulate empathy, or lead to the realizing of emotional truth. But when students encounter texts that do have these elements, they should consider applying the literary critic filter to gain enriched understanding. Using the literacy actions of *understanding* and flexibly *applying* any of these disciplinary literacy filters is the essence of academic literacy. An article from *Sports Illustrated* focusing on the career shifts of Bret Favre, longtime quarterback for the Green Bay Packers, or an Internet news article discussing the hazards of overcrowding in our nation's prisons, may seem completely out of context for the literary approach. Gearing up students to read like literary critics (Exhibit 2.9) would enable adolescents to develop sophisticated interpretations and understandings well beyond the norm. Isn't this, after all, the promise of teaching students to be literate in the disciplines?

EXHIBIT 2.9 **Disciplinary Literacy's Path of Action Gear for "READING LIKE A LITERARY CRITIC"**

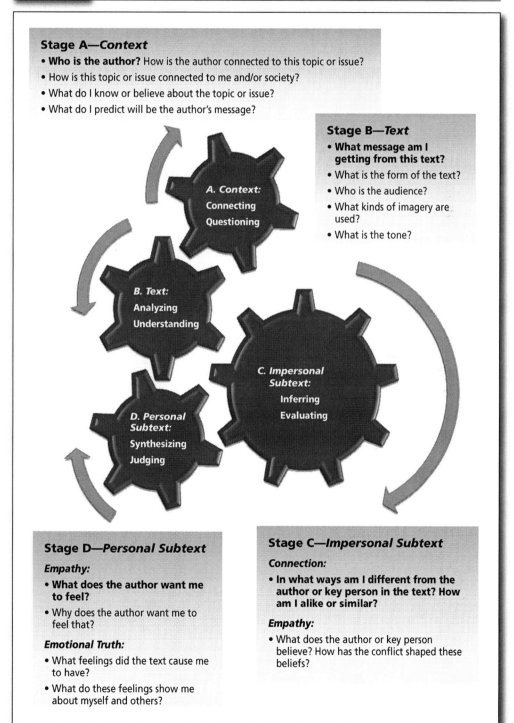

Stage A—*Context*
- **Who is the author?** How is the author connected to this topic or issue?
- How is this topic or issue connected to me and/or society?
- What do I know or believe about the topic or issue?
- What do I predict will be the author's message?

Stage B—*Text*
- **What message am I getting from this text?**
- What is the form of the text?
- Who is the audience?
- What kinds of imagery are used?
- What is the tone?

A. Context:
Connecting
Questioning

B. Text:
Analyzing
Understanding

C. Impersonal Subtext:
Inferring
Evaluating

D. Personal Subtext:
Synthesizing
Judging

Stage D—*Personal Subtext*

Empathy:
- **What does the author want me to feel?**
- Why does the author want me to feel that?

Emotional Truth:
- What feelings did the text cause me to have?
- What do these feelings show me about myself and others?

Stage C—*Impersonal Subtext*

Connection:
- **In what ways am I different from the author or key person in the text? How am I alike or similar?**

Empathy:
- What does the author or key person believe? How has the conflict shaped these beliefs?

READING LIKE A SCIENTIST

In our discussion of Disciplinary Literacy so far, we have examined two content areas from what is generally considered the humanities branch of academic pursuit. We are about to radically switch gears with our focus now on what it means to read like a scientist. Here, as with history and literature, we will not focus on the specific content of the various areas of scientific study. The focus is to uncover what it means to explore nonscientific text, even everyday text, as a scientist might. What might a scientist look for in an online news account of a "Breaking Headline News Story"? What is it that gives scientists insight that enables them to understand elements of texts that others miss? In short, how can an adolescent read like a scientist? We will address the question: What is it that scientists might seek as input when they read, and how could they transform that input into deeper understanding? In the realms of history and literature, we have centered our efforts on the literacy actions of *inferring* and *analyzing* assumptions and conclusions which cannot, in the strictest sense, be proven. A well-written essay asserting that Benjamin Franklin was a racist may make for captivating reading, but inferring the author's motive and intent as a historian does not rise to the level of scientific proof. Likewise, reading the same article may shock a reader into the realization—the *emotional truth*—that human judgment is often clouded by strong emotions, but this truth cannot be demonstrated in the science laboratory. Can we really say that the things historians and literary critics filter from text are untrue unless they can be proven through scientific demonstration? Must we conclude that motives, intentions, feelings, and emotional truths are *soft* knowledge, unworthy of much intellectual pursuit? Thankfully, no! But it is fair to say that the conclusions that may be drawn from reading as a historian or literary critic do not, and often cannot, rise to the level of scientific proof. "Science is one way of knowing about our world. The unspoken assumption behind all scientific endeavors is that general laws govern everything in the physical world" (Hazen and Trefil, 2009, p. 4). The implications of this "unspoken assumption" are that those laws are verifiable, through established facts, data collection, and demonstration. This in turn drives the ways in which scientists seek to "know" the world. Scientific theories are based on data, on hard facts, not on inferring feelings. In science, connections, feelings, and empathy are *not* keys to deeper understanding. Logical reasoning must rule the day.

Reading like a scientist awakens our students to seeing science in texts where they do not expect it.

The contribution of science to Disciplinary Literacy is its ability to awaken our students to seeing science in texts where they do not expect it. The key is for students to understand the critical benefit of reading like a scientist when they encounter text that has scientific content. So what does it mean to be scientifically literate? Hazen and Trefil define it this way: "For us, scientific literacy constitutes the knowledge you need to understand public issues.... If you can understand the news of the day as it relates to science, if you can take articles with headlines about stem cell research and the greenhouse effect and put them into a meaningful context—in short, if you can treat the news about science in the same way you treat everything else that comes over your horizon, then as far as we are concerned, you are scientifically literate" (2009, p. xiii). In the pursuit of teaching scientific knowledge, the elements of scientific thought that contribute to general literacy have been overlooked. Because of this, the adolescent student of science (or, for that matter, history, literature, mathematics, or music) is left with the impression that this content area is another isolated sphere of knowledge, or just "school stuff." Hazen and Trefil conclude, "the fact that you don't have to know how to design an airplane doesn't change the fact that you live in a world where airplanes exist, and your world is different because of them" (2009, p. xiii). The confusion on the part of many educators of science between the detailed pursuit of science and the elements of scientific literacy has left our students largely challenged scientifically. (And the same, again, may be said of history, literature, and even mathematics.) Our goal as educators must always be that all students will *do* science, and that they will *do* history, literature, and math also. But in the daily process of getting kids to *do*, we must admit that all of the kids we teach will not *be* scientists, historians, mathematicians, or writers someday. In short, they should be empowered by each discipline to be trustworthy citizen journalists.

Why Does Science Matter?

We must now, as we have done previously, examine how we can promote scientific literacy by understanding how a scientist might filter text to gain deeper understanding. We must address our ongoing question: What input do scientists seek from text, and how do they transform it into deeper understanding? And once again, we will focus on questioning text as the vehicle for gaining this deeper understanding at the context, text, and subtext levels. Before proceeding to the nuts and bolts of reading like a scientist, we need to take a few minutes to see why science matters as a field of academic pursuit. As with history and literature previously, we will examine three general arguments for the study of science in our schools, from the perspectives of civics, aesthetics, and intellectual connectedness.

Civics

No branch of academic pursuit has more immediate impact on our daily lives than does science. In a world of unrelenting technological advances, we are continually faced with new areas for scientific inquiry: Will nanotechnology usher in a paperless world, or make money obsolete? Growing out from the ever-expanding scientific inquiries are sometimes resulting dilemmas, including questions such as, "What will increased life expectancy do to the cost of health care?" This inquiry/dilemma relationship affects our daily lives through politics, law, public policy, and even our checkbook. Because of this, the discipline of science is more current as a course of study, perhaps, than at any previous time in our history. Being scientifically literate, then, is critical to informed citizenship.

Aesthetics

Science is not generally thought of as having artistic qualities. Science does not pursue beauty as an end in itself as the arts and some other academic content areas arguably do. But it does, in a sense, expose us to beauty. Understanding the relationships that science reveals to us provides us with a sense of artistic pleasure.

Intellectual Connectedness

Little of history or philosophy or current social policy may be fully understood without considering the impact of science. Indeed, scientific discovery has altered long-held notions of what is true and untrue in every age of the modern existence of human beings. Because of this, science is intimately connected to the other disciplines. By acknowledging the interconnectedness of science with history, literature, and mathematics, we better understand the world we live in.

What Do Scientists Seek to Know?

The scientist seeks different knowledge and insight than the historian or literary critic. "As a way of thinking, science has produced remarkable results. Its method of attempting to make sense of the universe we live in by not only asking questions, but going on to perform carefully organized data-generating experiments, has let humans look inside minute atoms as well as probe the vastness of space" (Moore, 2006, p. 6). The scientist seeks to reveal the truth of the physical world.

Disciplinary Literacy's Four-Stage Text Investigation: Reading Like a Scientist

We have seen how science differs from history and literature in its pursuit of understanding, and we have briefly discussed why science is a vital area of study for all students. We must now explore what reading like a scientist entails and how it can produce deeper understanding for students. As before, we will focus our investigation of text on the four levels: context, text, impersonal subtext, and personal sub-text. At each level, we will use questions to stimulate the deeper understanding we want our students to gain.

Context—Stage A

At the context level, it is important for students to con-nect the author to the topic written about in the text. In the Context Frame: Science (Exhibit 2.10), we will ask the same straightforward question that we did with his-tory and literature: "Who is the author and what scien-tific expertise does the author have?"

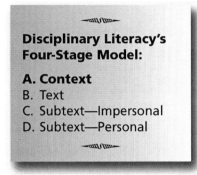

Disciplinary Literacy's Four-Stage Model:

A. Context
B. Text
C. Subtext—Impersonal
D. Subtext—Personal

What matters here is that students raise questions about how qualified the author might be in terms of the scientific issues raised by the text. A local reporter

EXHIBIT 2.10   Context Frame: Science

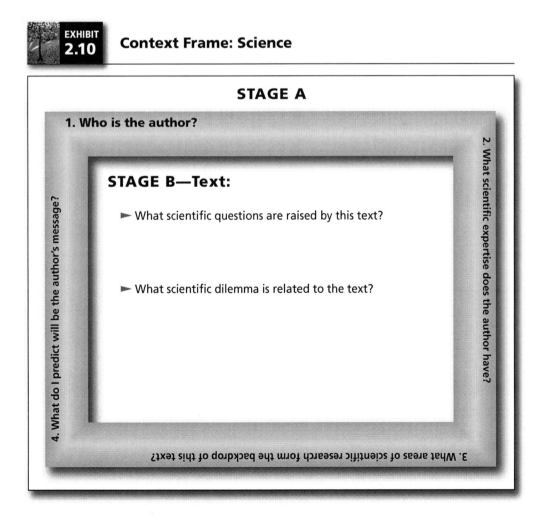

STAGE A

1. Who is the author?

STAGE B—Text:

► What scientific questions are raised by this text?

► What scientific dilemma is related to the text?

2. What scientific expertise does the author have?

4. What do I predict will be the author's message?

3. What areas of scientific research form the backdrop of this text?

who claims that the new Walmart will destroy the wildlife in the local park would not carry the same weight as a local biologist who makes the same claim. To gain credibility, the reporter would have to quote the biologist in the news story. Applying Habits of Mind to determine authors' authority on the topic and the level of their expertise, students begin inferring to shape their questioning and responses at the text and subtext levels. The next aspect of context is the connection to an established area of scientific research. Students conclude this by responding to the following: "What area(s) of scientific research forms the backdrop for this text?" For example, in an article about the impact of building a new Walmart in a rural area, the scientific backdrop may be impact on a local forest or wildlife, due to an increase in traffic. To read like a scientist, students must seek the connections to science that are not the central focus of the text. The term "backdrop" is used here to emphasize the scientific connections behind what is written. Connecting the topic of the text to areas of science they are familiar with focuses their reading on science connections. Finally, with the scientific context established, students add a personal response to the question, "What do I predict will be the author's message?" Responding to this question gives students a starting point for tracing the scientific questions or the scientific dilemma that may be embedded in the text.

Disciplinary Literacy's Four-Stage Model:

A. Context
B. Text
C. Subtext—Impersonal
D. Subtext—Personal

Text—Stage B

Constructing a context focuses the mind for the job of analyzing the text. Since our focus has been on scientific literacy, we are especially concerned that students understand the scientific underpinnings of the text. It is critical for students to filter text (Exhibit 2.10, Stage B) by answering two related questions: "What scientific questions are raised by this text?" and "What scientific dilemma is related to this text?" For the first question, students must search deeper than the general area of science they identified as the backdrop for the text. Here, they must search the text with an eye to the specific scientific questions it raises, directly or indirectly. Students might have identified the environment as the backdrop for the Walmart article mentioned earlier. Now their task would be to generate scientific evaluation questions, such as, "If rats are drawn to the area to feed from the dumpsters, could this spread disease?" By "scientific question," we mean a question with possible answers that can be supported with data from observation or experiment, or a question that is connected to existing areas of scientific research. We refer to these questions as "connected" because they may be raised by the text even though they are not discussed by the author. Similarly, students must ask themselves if there is a scientific dilemma—a problem defying a solution—connected to the text. Continuing with our Walmart example, a dilemma raised by the text may be, "How do we prevent the spread of disease to the local populations of humans and wildlife?" Uncovering this type of scientific dilemma related to a text is truly reading like a scientist. It is *using* science for a deeper understanding of text. Of course, students could also research the existing scientific knowledge—then they would be *doing* science.

The Context Frame for science gives students a place to respond briefly to the questions discussed above. As we have seen earlier, each context question forms one side of the frame, which surrounds the text questions placed in the center. This visual arrangement supports the relationship of context to the text itself. Stage A of the Context Frame: Science may be used with the same text as another discipline's Context Frame. If students can satisfactorily answer the context and text questions for different disciplines, they can see that the same text may be rich enough for reading as both a historian and a scientist. To filter a text from multiple perspectives reinforces the strength and flexibility of Disciplinary Literacy.

Impersonal Subtext—Stage C

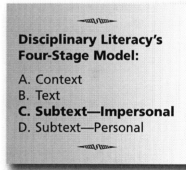

Disciplinary Literacy's Four-Stage Model:

A. Context
B. Text
C. Subtext—Impersonal
D. Subtext—Personal

Having covered the context and text, we now turn our attention to the subtext levels for reading like a scientist. Here, as with history and literature, students respond to questions that prompt them to read between the lines for deeper comprehension. At the impersonal subtext level, students are posed three related questions: 1) What scientific question or dilemma should be explored further? 2) How could this question be researched further? Here, students generate ideas about areas of science that could be researched that might shed light on the question or dilemma chosen. 3) What "thought experiment" can be developed to answer the question or resolve the dilemma? Students can respond to these questions on the Reading Like a Scientist Subtext Guide (Exhibit 2.11). A "thought experiment" is a thinking activity in which students design a scientific experiment on paper that, if conducted, could yield observable data that could be applied to answer the scientific question or resolve the dilemma chosen by them.

EXHIBIT 2.11 **Reading Like a Scientist Subtext Guide**

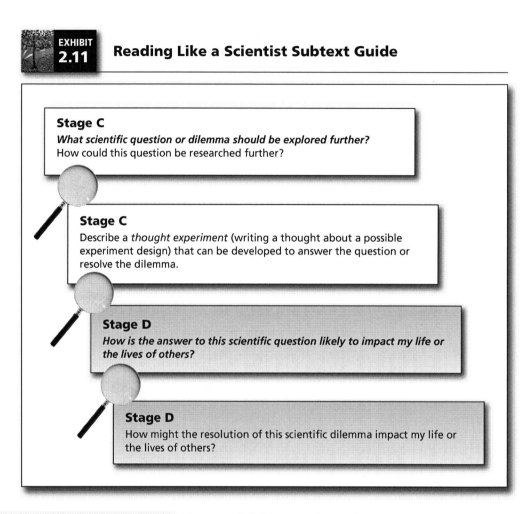

Stage C
What scientific question or dilemma should be explored further?
How could this question be researched further?

Stage C
Describe a *thought experiment* (writing a thought about a possible experiment design) that can be developed to answer the question or resolve the dilemma.

Stage D
How is the answer to this scientific question likely to impact my life or the lives of others?

Stage D
How might the resolution of this scientific dilemma impact my life or the lives of others?

Disciplinary Literacy's Four-Stage Model:

A. Context
B. Text
C. Subtext—Impersonal
D. Subtext—Personal

Personal Subtext—Stage D

At this level, students reflect on their previous thinking, and make personal connections by responding to two additional questions: "How is the answer to this scientific question likely to impact my life or the lives of others?" And, if a scientific dilemma has been identified, "How might the resolution of this dilemma impact my life or the lives of others?" Here, students apply the results of reading like a scientist on a personal level for themselves or others (Exhibit 2.11, Stage D). These questions are open-ended by design, targeting an area not often covered in a traditional science class. Students must *synthesize* their reading and thinking to develop their responses.

Gearing up literacy for reading like a scientist includes four stages of text investigation (Exhibit 2.12).

EXHIBIT 2.12

Disciplinary Literacy's Path of Action Gear for "READING LIKE A SCIENTIST"

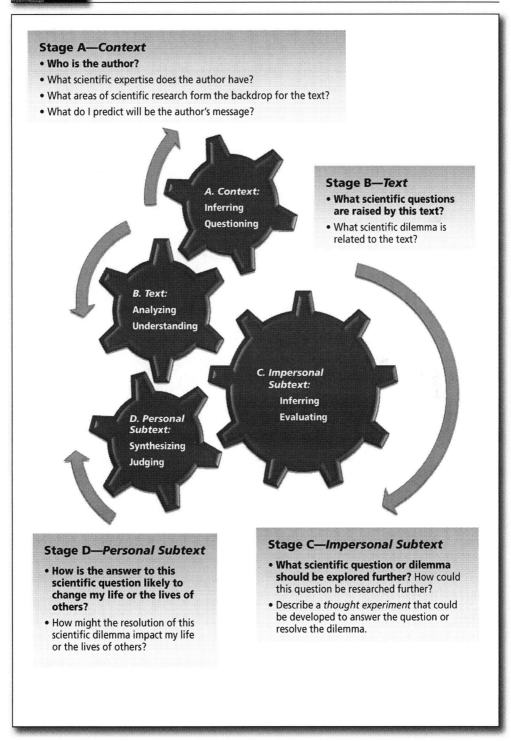

Stage A—*Context*
- **Who is the author?**
- What scientific expertise does the author have?
- What areas of scientific research form the backdrop for the text?
- What do I predict will be the author's message?

A. Context:
Inferring
Questioning

Stage B—*Text*
- **What scientific questions are raised by this text?**
- What scientific dilemma is related to the text?

B. Text:
Analyzing
Understanding

C. Impersonal Subtext:
Inferring
Evaluating

D. Personal Subtext:
Synthesizing
Judging

Stage D—*Personal Subtext*
- **How is the answer to this scientific question likely to change my life or the lives of others?**
- How might the resolution of this scientific dilemma impact my life or the lives of others?

Stage C—*Impersonal Subtext*
- **What scientific question or dilemma should be explored further?** How could this question be researched further?
- Describe a *thought experiment* that could be developed to answer the question or resolve the dilemma.

The Subtext Guide (Exhibit 2.11) prompts students to respond to each of the questions mentioned above. It is offered as a visual way to organize the questions students will respond to and give them an overview on a single page of the questions at the personal and impersonal levels. Its design should not limit the length and depth of students' responses. The organizer should be reviewed with students so that they understand how questions for the personal subtext are extensions of their responses for the impersonal subtext. Students may use the boxes to jot down notes for related areas of science to explore as research for their chosen scientific question, or to make a rough draft of their thought experiment.

READING LIKE A MATHEMATICIAN

Mathematics is one of the most intriguing areas of Disciplinary Literacy. Filtering text like a mathematician requires simplicity and clarity, which are valued qualities in mathematics. Math has been called the universal language. Indeed, it is a language without an alphabet. As such, what math communicates is not bound by culture or geographic region. Mathematical equations and formulas are as clear in Beijing as they are Washington D.C., without the necessity of translation. The often-heard comment, "Do the math," reflects the ability of mathematical logic to overturn common misconceptions.

"Doing the math" in the academic sense is a major part of every student's education. Yet, despite the many hours spent developing mathematical proficiency, students' ability to think like mathematicians has largely been lost. As Lockhart observed, "Mathematics is the art of explanation. If you deny students the opportunity to engage in this activity—to pose their own problems, to make their own conjectures and discoveries, to be wrong, to be creatively frustrated, to have an inspiration, and to cobble together their own explanations and proofs—you deny them mathematics itself" (2002, p. 5). It seems that, as with science, many students spend their time in math classes *doing* mathematics, instead of *using* mathematics. And *using* mathematics is precisely the ability that reading like a mathematician requires.

> *Using mathematics is precisely the ability that reading like a mathematician requires.*

Why Does Mathematics Matter?

Before we progress with how using math promotes literacy, we must look at why math is such an important discipline. To do so, we will again consider the topic from the perspectives of civics, aesthetics, and intellectual connectedness.

Civics

The ability to solve problems mathematically is central to daily life. At a time when the economy of the United States faces great challenges, many educators have proposed, even required, coursework for students in financial literacy. When individuals, corporations, or government agencies mishandle finances, the results can be disastrous for an entire nation, and perhaps for the entire world. What could be more critical to producing citizens who understand how to responsibly handle finances? These citizens will support the institutions and elect the government which will oversee finances at the national level. But beyond this, the ability to think mathematically promotes the development of informed citizens who possess Habits of Mind to calculate the consequences of both individual and collective actions and decisions, to evaluate the probability of success, and to create and use the technologies of the future.

Aesthetics

Mathematics is concerned with simplicity, elegance, and truth. The same may be said of other arts, such as music, literature, sculpture, and painting. Some mathematicians consider mathematics to be "the purest of the arts, as well as the most misunderstood" (Lockhart, 2002, p. 3). The idea that mathematics is an art may come as a surprise to most of us. Gowers notes, "It often puzzles people when mathematicians use words like *elegant*, *beautiful* or even *witty* to describe proofs. Music provides a useful analogy: we may be entranced when a piece moves in an unexpected harmonic direction that later comes to seem wonderfully appropriate, or when an orchestral texture appears to be more than the sum of its parts in a way that we do not fully understand. Mathematical proofs can provide similar pleasure, with sudden revelations, unexpected yet natural ideas, and intriguing hints that there is more to be discovered. Of course, beauty in mathematics is not the same as beauty in music, but neither is musical beauty the same as the beauty of a painting, or a poem, or a human face" (2002, p. 61). In the next discipline we will discuss, reading like a musician, we will see how math and music are inherently connected through math being the foundation of musical compositions. For all of its practicality and functionality, mathematics has an aesthetic aspect, conveying beauty to those with the eye to see it.

Intellectual Connectedness

Mathematical principles are part of the foundation of every field of academic pursuit. Artistic expression is difficult to analyze in music, painting, poetry, and literature without consideration of the mathematical elements of composition. From the

Great Pyramids to the Space Shuttle, applied mathematics has advanced the human condition. From the abacus to the personal computer, applied mathematics has improved and shaped our daily lives. The comprehension and application of mathematical principles are foundational to every field of human intellectual pursuit.

What Do Mathematicians Seek to Know?

Mathematics in its strictest sense is not satisfied with the use of inferring, even if the concepts are based on solid support or evidence. "Mathematicians are rarely satisfied with the phrase 'it seems that.' Instead, they demand a proof, which is an argument that puts a statement beyond all doubt" (Gowers, 2002, p. 43). It might be said, then, that mathematics as a way of knowing seeks absolute truth.

Disciplinary Literacy's Four-Stage Text Investigation: Reading Like a Mathematician

To read like a mathematician, students must be able to *use* math to question text. But before they can do that, students must be able to *see* math within the nonmath texts they read. Unfortunately, time spent in many math classrooms today leaves students blind to the fact that numbers and math are often key elements in other texts they read every day. In his bestselling book, *A Mathematician Reads the Newspaper*, Paulos explains, "because of the mind-numbing way in which mathematics is taught, many people have serious misconceptions about the subject and fail to appreciate its wide applicability" (1995, p. 3). Despite what many students are led to believe, Paulos continues, "It's time to let the secret out: Mathematics is not primarily a matter of plugging numbers into formulas and performing rote computations. It is a way of thinking and *questioning* that may be unfamiliar to many of us, but is available to almost all of us" (1995, p. 3). To use math to question text, Paulos asserts that students must look for what he calls the "number story" beneath the surface story of the text. Uncovering the number story in a text is simply identifying the ideas and claims made by an author that may be tested using mathematical principles and reasoning. The number story may be as simple as testing the claim that Sprint has the most 3G coverage. To read text as a mathematician, students must filter the text for details that point to the number stories beneath the words and sentences. Finally, they must explore how understanding the number story changes their comprehension of the text.

Context—Stage A

Once again, students begin to establish the context of what they read by answering the question, "Who is the author of the text, and how is he or she connected to the topic of the text?" As with science, connecting the author to the text is the first piece of evidence students can use while questioning the accuracy of the author's claims or ideas. To further establish the mathematical context of a text, students must move on to two additional questions: "What areas of mathematics are connected to this text?" and "What deeper meaning in the text could math reveal?" An article discussing the possible impact of the "Tea Party" movement as a third political party in future

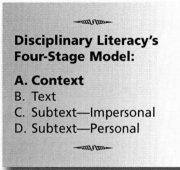

Disciplinary Literacy's Four-Stage Model:

A. Context
B. Text
C. Subtext—Impersonal
D. Subtext—Personal

presidential elections will most likely involve data from political polls. If so, statistical analysis would certainly be an area of mathematics connected to the text. Finally, students predict what they believe the message of the text will be, by answering the question, "What do I predict will be the author's message?" By responding to these context questions using the Context Frame: Mathematics (Exhibit 2.13), adolescents begin to construct the number story beneath the surface story of the text.

EXHIBIT 2.13 **Context Frame: Mathematics**

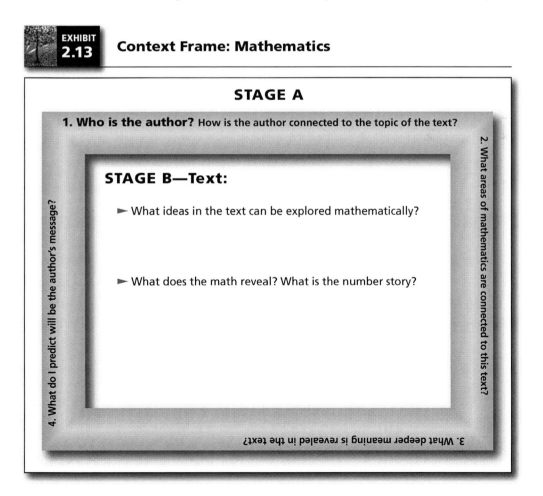

STAGE A

1. Who is the author? How is the author connected to the topic of the text?

2. What areas of mathematics are connected to this text?

STAGE B—Text:

► What ideas in the text can be explored mathematically?

► What does the math reveal? What is the number story?

4. What do I predict will be the author's message?

3. What deeper meaning is revealed in the text?

Disciplinary Literacy's Four-Stage Model:

A. Context
B. Text
C. Subtext—Impersonal
D. Subtext—Personal

Text—Stage B

At the text level, students continue to build the number story by filtering out those text details based on strong mathematical connections that lend themselves to mathematical analysis. Two general questions guide this process (Exhibit 2.13, Stage B): "What ideas or claims presented in the text can be explored mathematically?" and "What does the math reveal? What is the number story?" Possibilities for using math to *analyze* text include the following: Probability considerations can enhance articles about crime, health risks, and racial bias; business finance, the multiplication principle, and math processes point out sports myths. Once students have identified ideas and claims that may be analyzed mathematically, they are ready to infer what such analysis may reveal, which is the point of the second question. Here, the number story fully emerges.

Disciplinary Literacy's Four-Stage Model:

A. Context
B. Text
C. Subtext—Impersonal
D. Subtext—Personal

Impersonal Subtext—Stage C

At the subtext level, students combine what they have gleaned from responding to the questions at the context and text levels to evaluate the text in light of what the number story reveals on the Reading Like a Mathematician Subtext Guide (Exhibit. 2.14, Stage C).

Here, students must first consider the question, "How does mathematical analysis, or the number story, support or refute the author's ideas or claims?" One example might involve the so-called *availability error*—"the psychological disposition to begin *judging* and *evaluating* in light of the first thing that comes to mind (or is 'available' to the mind)" (Paulos, 1995, p. 15). An article about the state of the economy entitled "The Economic Holocaust" may predispose readers to accept claims made by the author based on their emotional reaction to the term "holocaust." If the author asserts within the same article that precious metals are the only safe investment at this time, fearful readers may have a tendency to agree, rather than questioning the logic. In this case, the number story may refute or validate the author's financial advice. Once the author's assertions have been measured against what the number story reveals, students then consider the question, "How does the number story deepen your understanding of the text?" Here students comment on the value of reading like a mathematician by applying their understanding of the relationship of the number story to the surface story of the text. In so doing, they validate for themselves the

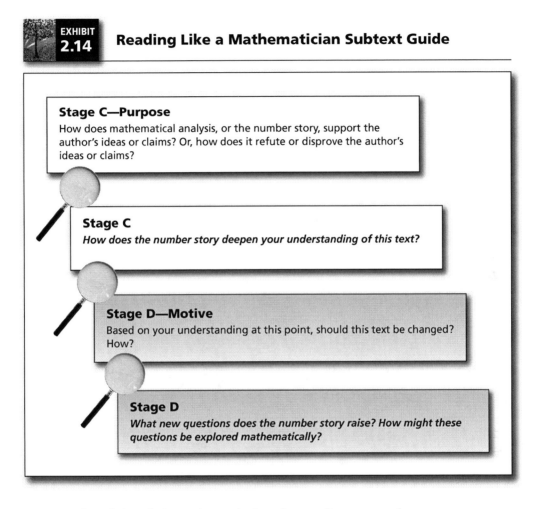

EXHIBIT 2.14 **Reading Like a Mathematician Subtext Guide**

Stage C—Purpose
How does mathematical analysis, or the number story, support the author's ideas or claims? Or, how does it refute or disprove the author's ideas or claims?

Stage C
How does the number story deepen your understanding of this text?

Stage D—Motive
Based on your understanding at this point, should this text be changed? How?

Stage D
What new questions does the number story raise? How might these questions be explored mathematically?

process of applying their mathematical understanding to text that may not appear to have any direct connection to mathematics.

Personal Subtext—Stage D

At this final level of text investigation, students extend their understanding of the number story beyond the text (Exhibit 2.14, Stage D). First, students are asked to consider changes they would make to the text given what the number story has revealed to them through the question, "Based on your understanding at this point, should this text be changed? How?" Here students are synthesizing their mathematical analysis of the text with their personal judgment of the author's work. As students extend what they learned from reading like a

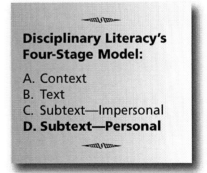

Disciplinary Literacy's Four-Stage Model:

A. Context
B. Text
C. Subtext—Impersonal
D. Subtext—Personal

EXHIBIT 2.15

Disciplinary Literacy's Path of Action Gear for "READING LIKE A MATHEMATICIAN"

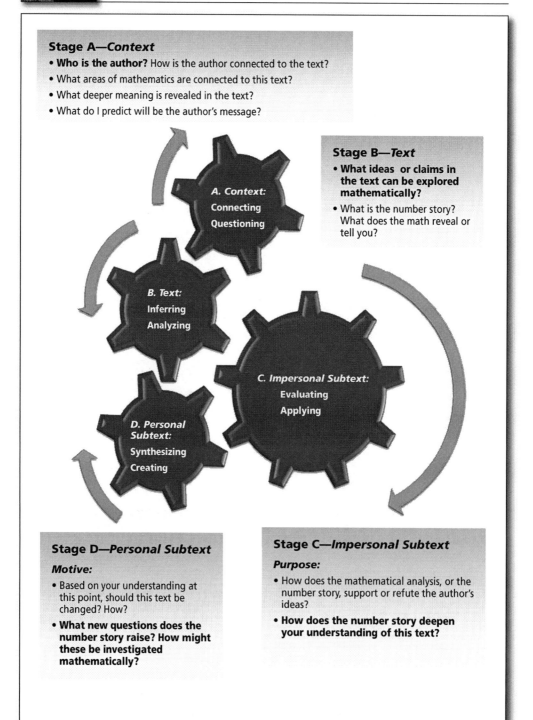

Stage A—*Context*
- **Who is the author?** How is the author connected to the text?
- What areas of mathematics are connected to this text?
- What deeper meaning is revealed in the text?
- What do I predict will be the author's message?

Stage B—*Text*
- **What ideas or claims in the text can be explored mathematically?**
- What is the number story? What does the math reveal or tell you?

A. Context:
Connecting
Questioning

B. Text:
Inferring
Analyzing

C. Impersonal Subtext:
Evaluating
Applying

D. Personal Subtext:
Synthesizing
Creating

Stage D—*Personal Subtext*

Motive:
- Based on your understanding at this point, should this text be changed? How?
- **What new questions does the number story raise? How might these be investigated mathematically?**

Stage C—*Impersonal Subtext*

Purpose:
- How does the mathematical analysis, or the number story, support or refute the author's ideas?
- **How does the number story deepen your understanding of this text?**

mathematician, they reinforce the power of applying mathematics in daily life and creating with the questions "What new questions does the number story raise?" and "How might these questions be explored mathematically?" Reading like a mathematician requires students to uncover the story that the numbers tell and to evaluate what has been written in light of that story, as represented by Disciplinary Literacy's Path of Action Gear for Reading Like a Mathematician (Exhibit 2.15). It is important to note that the process of reading like a mathematician is available to all students, regardless of their skill level in math. However, the simplicity of the questions may be deceptive: uncovering the number story may require quite an in-depth understanding of mathematics. Be that as it may, the power of seeking the *number story beneath the surface story* pushes students to *use* math, instead of only *doing* math. And how can any of our students, even the most mathematically challenged, afford to face their future without this ability?

READING LIKE A MUSICIAN: CONNECTING HISTORIANS, LITERARY CRITICS, SCIENTISTS, AND MATHEMATICIANS

Conversations fuel literacy understanding. Intentional conversations focused on literacy have a source of energy and discovery. Many dialogues have led to the understanding that the very essence of literacy resides within teachers of the arts. Although integrating the curriculum has been encouraged in recent years, strong expectations for curricular integration between English language arts and the disciplines of history/social studies and science have been established by the Common Core State Standards. Yet, it has been musicians who have been naturally making literacy connections for centuries.

> *Musicians have been naturally making literacy connections for centuries.*

READING LIKE A MUSICIAN

There is a unique relationship between connections that exist with language, math, science, history, and culture, and being an excellent music teacher. These connections were conveyed in 1903 by a French music professor, Albert Lavignac (1922), when he explained, "Music is a sort of universal language, as it excites emotions and stimulates the intellect. It reflects the continuously changing cultures in all countries."

Why Does Music Matter?

Never was the universal language characteristic of music more poignant than during Haiti's Port-au-Prince earthquake. An article in the *Washington Post* described the scene: "At night, voices rise in the street. Sweet, joyful, musical voices in lyric Creole. A symphony of hope in a landscape of despair" (Roig-Franzia, 2010). The religious and cultural differences of thousands were blended together in their misery as they questioned, "Why was I spared?" In the midst of traumatic cultural change, united Haitians spoke to the world through music. This devastating event embodied the importance of music from the civics perspective as it united courage. The aesthetic beauty of music can contribute a depth of understanding to intellectual connections. Filling the spaces within hearts broken by lives empty of hope, music seeped inside the pain to massage grief. Razor-sharp edges of pain were dulled as the magic of music cushioned humanity's despair.

What Do Musicians Seek to Know?

What is it about music that establishes natural *connections*? Music has been the model for integrating the curriculum, from incorporating fluency while reading scores during playing and singing music to using math concepts while composing and reading music. Additionally, it is not surprising that music transcends learning by impacting relationships, as some of our most moving conversations with, and gifts from, the hearts of our own children have been centered on music.

Disciplinary Literacy's Four-Stage Text Investigation: Reading Like a Musician

What can we learn from music's transcendence throughout all of life? The Context Frame: Music (Exhibit 2.16) guides connections for establishing comprehension of the context and the text beginning with considering how music reflects the culture. The writing style of the composer is considered in the text investigation.

Reading like a musician includes incorporating the subtext by reflecting on how the composer was able to captivate the intellect of the instrumentalist (the "reader"). Questioning how the composer "charmed the ear" of the reader leads to considering how an inner conflict may have influenced the composition. While reading Lavignac's (1922, p. 6) explanation, "Music is then at once a language...," we discussed how music provides a gift—a window into the heart of adolescents and our own children.

To understand how each discipline is an integral component in the study of music, we will use the music filter to read like a musician. A significant structural difference of reading like a musician compared to other disciplines is when a musician transfers the reading attributes needed for reading musical texts (written as sheet music) to texts in different disciplines, the transfer *automatically applies to any text*

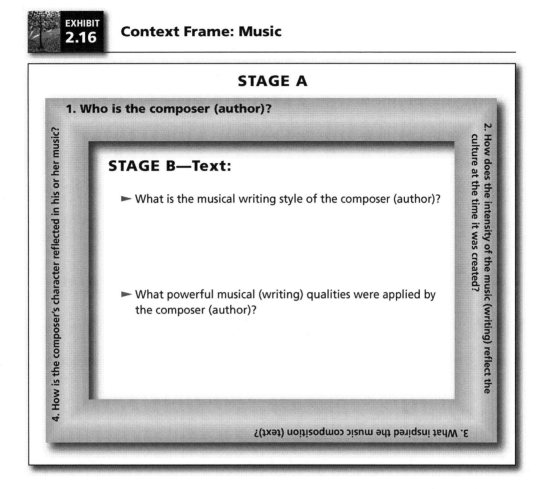

EXHIBIT 2.16 **Context Frame: Music**

STAGE A

1. Who is the composer (author)?

STAGE B—Text:

➤ What is the musical writing style of the composer (author)?

➤ What powerful musical (writing) qualities were applied by the composer (author)?

4. How is the composer's character reflected in his or her music?

2. How does the intensity of the music (writing) reflect the culture at the time it was created?

3. What inspired the music composition (text)?

in all disciplines. "Text" read by musicians (sheet music) is not a standard genre of writing. Therefore, the filter for reading like a musician in different disciplines is a global and more encompassing filter. Two guiding questions led us to deeper understanding: "Can the filter for reading like a musician be applied by those from other disciplines who are not musicians?" and "Can the musician filter improve comprehension within different disciplines?" Those outside the discipline of music cannot read as a musician in the music discipline unless they are trained in reading sheet music. This point contrasts to filters such as history that enable nonhistorians to read history like historians. Therefore, is it beneficial for the music filter to be applied to other disciplines? Remember, the music filter immediately transfers to *all* disciplines since the limitations of sheet music exist only within the field of music.

Just as we have discussed in the previous disciplines, applying a discipline filter to read in different contents increases understanding. Once outside the realm of music, the music filter applies to all disciplines equally. For example, nonmusicians

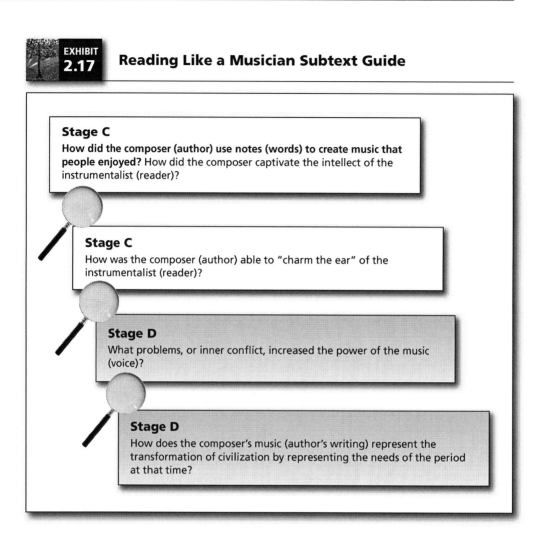

EXHIBIT 2.17   Reading Like a Musician Subtext Guide

Stage C
How did the composer (author) use notes (words) to create music that people enjoyed? How did the composer captivate the intellect of the instrumentalist (reader)?

Stage C
How was the composer (author) able to "charm the ear" of the instrumentalist (reader)?

Stage D
What problems, or inner conflict, increased the power of the music (voice)?

Stage D
How does the composer's music (author's writing) represent the transformation of civilization by representing the needs of the period at that time?

cannot comprehend sheet music more deeply by using a music filter, because sheet music is a language they do not understand. However, we can use the musician filter that evolved out of necessity to read texts in *all* disciplines. This explains why musicians are, at once, mathematicians, scientists, historians, linguists, and artists. Musicians cannot limit the use of their musician filter to their own discipline, because they *accept* that they must comprehend other disciplines to teach their own. Their music filter is naturally applied *out of necessity*. Historians can *choose* to apply their history filter when reading other disciplines, because the language is not a barrier. The previous disciplinary filters for each subject are not limited to a specific content, but can be applied when reading different disciplines. It's a two-way street.

What musician qualities connect with different disciplines? As in literature, music is powerful in its capacity to convey intensity of feelings—a direct line to emotions and source of inspiration. Like history, music represents culture through

EXHIBIT 2.18 Disciplinary Literacy's Path of Action Gear for "READING LIKE A MUSICIAN" Connecting History, Language, Science, and Mathematics

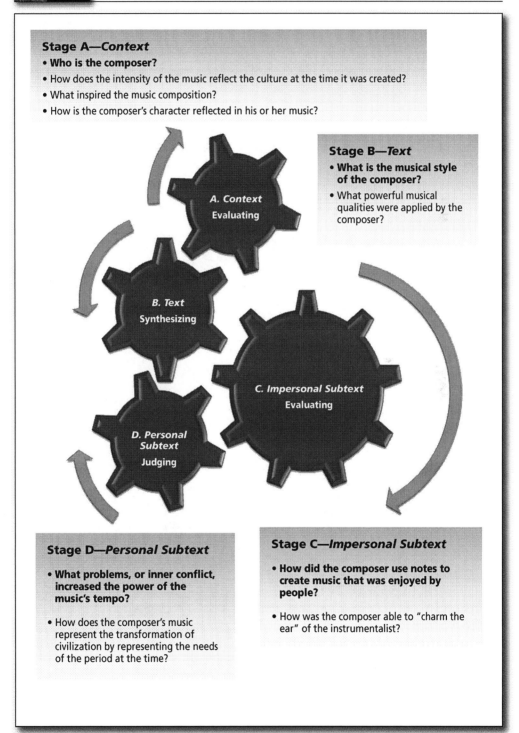

Stage A—*Context*
- **Who is the composer?**
- How does the intensity of the music reflect the culture at the time it was created?
- What inspired the music composition?
- How is the composer's character reflected in his or her music?

Stage B—*Text*
- **What is the musical style of the composer?**
- What powerful musical qualities were applied by the composer?

A. Context
Evaluating

B. Text
Synthesizing

C. Impersonal Subtext
Evaluating

D. Personal Subtext
Judging

Stage D—*Personal Subtext*
- **What problems, or inner conflict, increased the power of the music's tempo?**
- How does the composer's music represent the transformation of civilization by representing the needs of the period at the time?

Stage C—*Impersonal Subtext*
- **How did the composer use notes to create music that was enjoyed by people?**
- How was the composer able to "charm the ear" of the instrumentalist?

expressions and the slang of the times. As with mathematics, values in music are vital: a quarter note cannot be mistaken for a whole note, or the end result will be flawed. Science provides the rationale for achieving the greatest performance capacity from each instrument.

Learning language and music occurs naturally while growing up, and also formally in school through instruction about theory. Disciplinary Literacy's Path of Action Gear for Reading Like a Musician (Exhibit 2.18) provides guiding questions for this topic. Music is a pure discipline available to all listeners, not dependent upon books, equations, or science labs. As Lavignac (1922, p. 4) explained, although it is an art, musicians do not need a canvas to "Charm the ear, interest the mind and sometimes elevate the soul."

Chapter 2 Conclusion

Dear Readers,

Disciplinary Literacy as an instructional approach has sprouted from the "reading in the content areas" movement. Instead of asking what reading practices can and should be transplanted into history, literature, science, math, and music classes to improve student comprehension, it honors the contents, asking instead what they each, as invaluable components of a secondary education, have to offer adolescents for comprehension of texts they encounter in their daily lives. We have examined how inverting our old approach to content reading can energize students, giving them valid reasons to quest for deeper comprehension, and even generating new interest in texts that may not have held their interest before. We can never predict with true certainty what our students will need to know in the future, but it is our duty to equip them for how they will gain the knowledge they need. To do this is to prepare them to become responsible citizen journalists. Is there anything more critical than this?

Sincerely,

Brian

CHAPTER 3

Disciplined Practice: A Literacy Leadership Model

H
ow does the literacy leadership model of Disciplined Practice support and *enhance the leader's capacity to learn and the learner's capacity to lead*? One goal of systems and organizations is to maintain homeostasis within an evolving culture and changing environment. Systems and organizations possess the desire to improve, but not all possess the leadership capacity to achieve ultimate literacy goals. Public education, as noted in previous chapters, did not successfully prepare 20th-century leaders or learners to meet exploding literacy needs in a dynamic multicultural population with social, fiscal, and racial divides. Disciplined Practice presents a literacy leadership model which connects the work of leaders, actions of teachers, and achievement of students. As the Carnegie Corporation's report for advancing adolescent literacy explains, "critical thinking and effective communication has to be at the center of everyone's efforts" (Carnegie Corporation, 2010, p. viii).

It is through Disciplined Practice that we are able to model Gardner's premise that "respectful and ethical minds cannot be outsourced" (2009). Specifically, as leaders, we cannot continue to outsource literacy. The Disciplined Practice Model for Literacy Leadership (Exhibit 3.1) is a framework for literacy improvement that integrates literacy and leadership actions.

The four phases of the Disciplined Practice Leadership Model are based on a cycle of improvement, as are other educational models, such as White's Leadership Maps (2009). Literacy actions, as the interlocking teeth of leadership gears, connect leadership with instructional decisions. Schools and systems have been using variations of the cycle of improvement to facilitate strategic, operational, and systemic change from the mid-1970s to the present. The Disciplined Practice model of the cycle of continuous improvement powers dynamic systemic and school connections. Disciplined Practice provides a common language using the literacy actions described in Chapter 1, with instructional practices described in Chapter 2, to support literacy leadership to guide literacy change within classrooms, schools, and across the system. Just as Lapp, Flood, Heath, and Langer explain, "Revising what

EXHIBIT 3.1 Disciplined Practice Model for Literacy Leadership

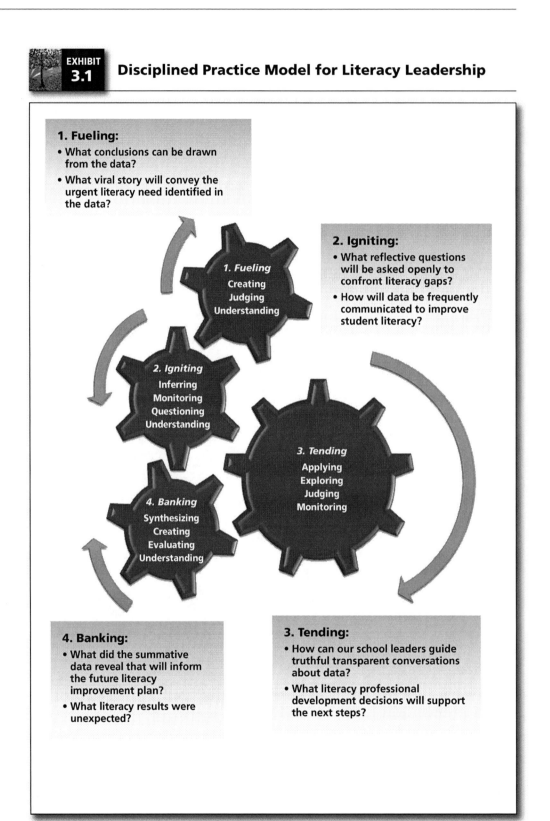

1. Fueling:
- What conclusions can be drawn from the data?
- What viral story will convey the urgent literacy need identified in the data?

2. Igniting:
- What reflective questions will be asked openly to confront literacy gaps?
- How will data be frequently communicated to improve student literacy?

1. Fueling

Creating
Judging
Understanding

2. Igniting

Inferring
Monitoring
Questioning
Understanding

3. Tending

Applying
Exploring
Judging
Monitoring

4. Banking

Synthesizing
Creating
Evaluating
Understanding

4. Banking:
- What did the summative data reveal that will inform the future literacy improvement plan?
- What literacy results were unexpected?

3. Tending:
- How can our school leaders guide truthful transparent conversations about data?
- What literacy professional development decisions will support the next steps?

we mean by all terms connected with literacy will come with greatest difficulty for institutions of formal school and their core constituents . . . administrators, teachers etc." (2009, p. 11), literacy actions are expanded to embody different roles, including guiding leadership decisions.

WHAT IS THE DISCIPLINED PRACTICE MODEL OF LITERACY LEADERSHIP?

The four phases of Disciplined Practice are fueling, igniting, tending, and banking. The same literacy actions applied in the classroom for teaching and learning are equally robust when specifically applied to these four phases of literacy leadership. The rationale for integrating literacy actions into leadership is to connect leadership and teacher practice in the cycle of school and system improvement. Literacy actions provide strong teeth that mesh the gears of improvement and personalize professional development. The exquisiteness of literacy actions demonstrates their capacity and flexibility to inform teacher instructional decisions, deepen student understanding, and inform decisions leaders make to promote building and system improvement.

The four phases of Disciplined Practice drive a cycle of improvement which crosses vertical and horizontal boundaries from the classroom to the boardroom. The Common Core State Standards (2010) provide opportunities for states, systems, schools, and classrooms to align transparent systemic improvement. The four phases of Disciplined Practice add value to Common Core State Standards conversations for teachers, administrators, and board members by providing a context for literacy change. Actionable processes, observable indicators, measurable goals, and specific outcomes created by Data Teams complete the cycle of improvement. The following four-phase improvement cycle is capable of facilitating systemic improvement in literacy. Scenarios include rural districts, suburban districts, and urban districts. The urban lower socioeconomic district scenarios and insights are provided by Dr. Brenda Conley, former Assistant Superintendent of Baltimore City Schools.

FUELING—PHASE 1 (INSERTING OXYGEN)

Nature provides excellent analogies for understanding the complexities of leadership. One example nature provides us is what occurs when natural phenomena are ignored. An example of natural phenomena left untended is the accumulation of undergrowth on the hillsides and ravines of the arid land near populated areas. The result is a potentially dangerous situation. Undergrowth left untended creates a serious risk of wildfires. Southwestern wildfires, notorious for their unpredictable path, spectacular flames, intense heat, and wanton destruction of property, mimic many of the behaviors educational systems produce when school or systemic change is implemented in an erratic manner. New leadership and mandated instructional models frequently avoid participant feedback, leaving questions unattended, which exacerbates the serious risk of initiative failure.

Hillsides and ravines within schools and systems are cleared of untended accumulations of system behaviors (undergrowth) through a focused change by incorporating specific literacy actions into leadership conversations. Pruned and grubbed landscapes benefit from intentional improvement cycles. The leader's role is to use data generated by Data Teams as fuel to facilitate the school's or system's cycle of improvement efforts. The fueling stage consists of applying data-based conclusions, like oxygen to a spark, to power the cycle of improvement. The leader collaboratively prepares an honest conclusion of the available data, noting various challenges and concerns. During the fueling phase, a viral story is created capable of generating participant commitment to act. A viral story describes urgent needs as they relate directly to students' lives. Validated data secures the viral story and justifies why the need must be addressed by the school or district. The viral story provides credence, generates support, and ensures participant commitment, because it connects with a deep sense of purpose residing within us, waiting to be awakened. The key to a viral story is typically the connection between identified student needs and the unique gifts of teachers. An example of a viral story is a superintendent asked a group of elementary English Language Learner students to share their future dreams. Students wrote letters to their middle school teachers to explain what they needed in middle school to achieve their dreams, and asked those teachers for help with learning. These students were monitored throughout middle and into high school. Their success story has become a book that is infecting others with their story of hope and enthusiasm, and is providing opportunities for replication throughout the country (Routman, 2010). Whether adding fuel to a system, school, or one student's life, viral stories hold within them the potential to connect with a calling.

> *The fueling stage consists of applying data-based conclusions, like oxygen to a spark, to power the cycle of improvement.*

The fueling process tests the ability of leaders to engage participants, teams, and professional learning communities in addressing an identified mission or critical need specific to the success of the school or system. The fueling stage contributes to the high understanding of antecedents in the "Learning" quadrant of the Leadership and Learning Matrix (Besser, Almeida, Anderson-Davis, Flach, Kamm, and White, 2008). Participant commitment to an identified need is assembled through the leader's capacity to facilitate collaborative engagement in specific literacy actions, including *creating, judging,* and *understanding.*

Creating (*generating a new point of view by combining different components*)

Creating is a literacy action used in the fueling phase of Disciplined Practice, guiding the leader to facilitate the interpretation of summative assessment data reports into a conclusion. The conclusion of summative assessment data creates motivation for the viral story to sustain participant commitment to the school's and the system's cycle of improvement. Based on conclusions drawn from the data, needs identified from within the school, system, or community that are critical to the success of the mission cannot be disregarded without causing irreparable harm to participant values or beliefs. Is this too strong a statement? Perhaps, unless it is understood that the failure of an improvement effort occurs when the need for action is not clearly communicated, understood, or openly agreed upon. A lack of focus cripples success, as evidenced in the following scenario.

Scenario for Creating: Teacher Performance or Student Opportunities

While collaborating with a frustrated elementary principal, I inquired, "Why is it so difficult for the school to meet the adopted improvement goals?"

The principal explained, "Conversations with the staff are very difficult to hold. Teachers don't want to face what they are not doing, but instead want me to tell them what they are to do."

I asked the principal how she responded when asked by teachers, "What do you want me to do?"

The principal said, "I usually ask the teacher where they believe they need to improve. Their response is generally, 'I don't know. This group of kids does not perform well on tests.'"

Situations like this occur in schools struggling to maintain or improve achievement. The principal and central office administrators do not have the answers. The fueling phase develops an inclusive process which does not presume to have the answers to these and other improvement questions, but which provides opportunities to face challenges the school must work to overcome. In contrast, the principal in another school with similar improvement challenges shared her viral story with me. When I asked, "How did you bring your teachers, parents, and students together around your school improvement goals for literacy?" she explained, "We gathered all of the data we believed to be relevant for literacy improvement. We created time to openly discuss what was working and what was not working for the students. We dropped what was not working and creatively focused upon what was working."

The difference between these two leadership scenarios is that the first scenario focused upon the teachers' ability to perform, and the second focused upon the students' opportunities to learn. The fueling phase focuses upon student learning, not teacher performance. The difference in focus permits teachers, parents, and administrators to look critically at student data, which will result in changes in teacher decisions. The key to the fueling process resides within the leader's ability to construct a base of participant commitment to specific critical needs. Participant support and commitment to identified needs is assembled through use of literacy actions. As Hattie explains, "Enhancing learning also needs school leaders and teachers who can create school, staff room, and classroom environments where teachers can talk about their teaching, where errors or difficulties are seen as critical learning opportunities, where discarding incorrect knowledge and understandings is welcomed, and where teachers can feel safe to learn, relearn..." (2009, p. 37).

Judging (*slowing down to make a transparent decision based on evidence, while acknowledging opinion*)

Judging is a literacy action used during the fueling phase that requires the leader to present conflicting points of view, honing participant focus. Leaders focusing on conclusions drawn from data require participants to challenge professional beliefs, question established policies, investigate accepted positions, and create new applications.

If accomplished successfully, judging infuses respect for the leader and advocacy for the participants. The leader is judged by participants when the presentation of the viral story sparks participant reflection and cooperation. Also, leaders are judged by the ability they demonstrate and the courage they exhibit in difficult situations. Judging influences the direction, focus, and participant commitment to the improvement plan. The success of the improvement plan and the leader's ability to continue as the leader is determined in the fueling phase.

Understanding (*explaining meaning; identifying how new initiatives improve performance*)

Understanding is a literacy action in the fueling phase that requires the leader to collectively and collaboratively devote energy, time, effort, and resources to address a common need. Understanding identifies, defines, and acknowledges the purpose propelling participant actions to address school and system needs. For example, understanding is demonstrated when leaders are able to support requests to acquire additional resources to address specific needs. Resources are continually a challenge in school and system literacy improvement efforts. Locating literacy resources requires the leader and participants to address the realities of their current situation in fiscal, human, time, and level of expertise areas. It is important to provide situational leadership for addressing resource concerns and issues. A strong fueling phase builds a foundation of enormous potential for the igniting phase. There is a need for a deeper level of understanding about how we learn, how we approach our work, and how we transfer that learning to others.

Scenario for Understanding: Identifying and Explaining Suggested Solutions for Improvement

The following conversation occurred while collaborating with a high school in one of the nation's largest school districts. This school district, which has more than 100,000 students, is described as "urbanizing"—experiencing significant change in student demographics. Of its 30 high schools, 80 percent have been targeted for "school improvement," a label of failure. One of those high schools had a new principal. In fact, he was the sixth new principal in five years. In his enthusiasm, he wanted to open every door to determine all the problems awaiting him. At the fueling phase, I encouraged him to determine key areas of focus and set an aligned direction for his staff by incorporating a viral story and including the specific literacy actions of *analyzing* the depth of concerns and *understanding* connections to identify the most appropriate human resources.

When the fueling phase of Disciplined Practice is not overlooked, but intentionally prepared, the igniting phase is aligned for success.

IGNITING—PHASE 2 (CREATING A SPARK)

The igniting phase of Disciplined Practice incorporates the conclusions drawn from data together with the viral story from the fueling phase to spark literacy changes needed in the school improvement plan. Professional wildfire fighters map out, within yards, the path of the burn they think a fire will follow, the intensity of the flame, and where firebreaks can be placed to deter the path of the burn. Once an improvement plan is mapped out and ignited, the leader and participants are able to monitor its path of progress through predictions for improvement defined in the SMART goals (Specific, Measureable, Attainable, Relevant, Timely). The leader's role in the igniting phase is to guide the integration of data identified by Data Teams into the improvement plan. The igniting phase frames the construction of the improvement plan.

Providing support for innovation and risk taking may be inherent in leaders, but it is not inherent throughout organizations. Schools and systems are organized to enforce compliance. Raising literacy expectations, igniting transformational change, shattering outmoded literacy mental models, melting historic paradigms, and changing daily literacy practice is easier discussed than accomplished during the launch of a cycle of improvement (Houston, Blankenstein, and Cole, 2009). Literacy actions that support the igniting phase of Disciplinary Practice include *questioning*, *monitoring*, *understanding*, and *inferring*.

Questioning (*leads to making appropriate decisions and solving problems effectively*)

The leader is responsible for forming, posing, and reframing reflective questions for participants to identify and verify that planned actions are focused upon the adopted goals. The leader's reflective questioning supports aligning practice and processes with the adopted goals. The leader's ability to reflectively question participants creates opportunities to stop the process, identify gaps, create learning opportunities, modify practice, and revise improvement goals. The leader in all phases of Disciplined Practice must use reflective practice to monitor progress, synthesize meaning, and create new understanding. Questioning is critical to the plan's success. Questioning works both ways: leaders pose questions for participants, and the leaders must be open to being questioned about their ability to lead, the actions they have taken, the results they have presented, and their evaluation of participant ability to respond and revisit issues. Leaders may feel threatened when participants ask questions openly in front of peers regarding actions taken, results interpreted, and funds expended, as demonstrated in the following scenario.

Scenario for Questioning: Powerful Questions Resolve Problems

The igniting phase embraces reflective questioning. In a meeting between the superintendent and the principal of an elementary school on the verge of reconstitution by the state department of education, questions were posed and directed both ways.

Superintendent: "Why hasn't the money spent on your school improved teacher instruction and student performance?"

Principal: "Our school has not been given clear and explicit directions and guidance from either the state education department or the central office on the specific needs we have to correct."

Superintendent: "Your scores are the lowest in the system and among the lowest in the state in reading, math, and science. What more direction do you require?"

Principal: "Our students come from the poorest parts of the county, our school is in the worst state of repair, and it serves as a revolving door for the least experienced or poorest performing teachers. What do you expect me to do under these conditions?"

Superintendent: "I want you to improve your school."

Principal: "I don't teach a class! How do I improve our school?"

That two-way conversation occurred in my presence. I did not see real progress come out of the dialogue; it resulted in more frustration and confusion. After the meeting, the superintendent said, "Do you see what I have to put up with?" A week later, the principal said, "I can't do anything right in his eyes. He blames me for everything that happens in this school." Conversations, when not data-driven, become unfocused. Conversations, when not job-embedded, become eclectic and unproductive.

Before my next visit, I asked the superintendent to compose a list of questions he would like to have answered by the principal. I sent the principal the list of questions and asked that they be presented to the school improvement team.

The three of us met three weeks later. The questions opened the conversation and the responses from the principal and school improvement team framed the discussion. The igniting phase of Disciplined Practice requires questions.

The most frustrating part of the igniting phase is addressing questions the leader assumes have been adequately answered. Leaders frequently trust that once a problem has been defined and an action determined, the problem can be forgotten. Issues and problems do not go away when they are not addressed. They go underground. Effective leaders keep problems in focus, continually monitor progress, and use data to frame conversations. Determining where the level of authority exists to make specific decisions is determined in the igniting phase. When responsibility for deciding who makes which decisions is not clearly delineated, the improvement plan is in jeopardy of slipping into complacency or falling into chaos. When the level of decision making leaders assume, and participants are delegated to make, is clearly defined in the igniting phase, the improvement process functions efficiently, as depicted in the recent CNN health update described below.

> *Issues and problems do not go away when they are not addressed. They go underground.*

Scenario for Questioning:
Decisions Require Questions

During a CNN Medical Update segment hosted by Dr. Sanjay Gupta on March 8, 2010, Dr. Peter Pronovost of Johns Hopkins University School of Medicine was interviewed about the topic of his book, "Safe Patients, Smart Hospital" (Gupta, 2010). Dr. Gupta asked, "Do nurses ask the operating physician, before the operation begins, have you washed your hands?"

Dr. Pronovost replied, "No. The doctor would tell the nurse, 'screw you.'"

The interview went on to explain that 31,000 patients die every year of infections introduced during hospital or physicians' office visits. Questions need to be asked. However, the culture of schools, hospitals, and businesses does not recognize or construct decision-sharing authority models. Dr. Pronovost went on to explain that the purpose for creating a checklist in hospital operating rooms is to have an agreed-upon protocol in place to prevent mistakes, identify failures, and even minimize the occurrence of untimely deaths (Gupta, 2010).

Questioning is a critical component of every practice, and especially Disciplined Practice. Reflective questioning supports leadership, inspiring creativity and risk taking, as shown in Exhibits 3.2 and 3.3. These charts guide literacy questions at school and district levels.

Monitoring (*determining progress and addressing limiting factors*)

Monitoring is the literacy action requiring leaders to continually check the pulse of participant commitment. Monitoring identifies and confirms administrator and participant agreements while uncovering gaps. Monitoring defines the scope of the professional development plan needed to improve school and system performance. The igniting phase engages leaders and participants in reflective practice and opens opportunities to identify actions to improve school and system performance. Monitoring engages leaders and participants in honest and transparent conversations to support the cycle of improvement.

Scenario for Monitoring:
Removing Limiting Factors to Improve Student Progress

A statement that we hear over and over again in a multitude of struggling urban schools is, "What you are presenting seems very useful, but that would never work here." Responding to such statements always includes the simple question, "Why?"

EXHIBIT 3.2

Literacy Leadership Questioning for *School-Based* Administrators

Beginning of the Year	During the Year	End of the Year
1. How many students in your class are performing below and on or above their enrolled grade-level standards? Who are these students—what are their names?	7. If you could start this quarter all over, what would you do differently? How can I help you make this happen during this marking period?	13. How much progress did each student make with you this year?
2. This is your moment to hold the baton of student progress! At what level are you beginning instruction with this student?	8. What new goals do you have for below-grade-level students? How will you determine students' progress?	14. What instructional interventions had the greatest impact on your students' progress this year? What will you do differently next year?
3. At what reading or math level did *last* year's teacher recommend that this student begin *this* year?	9. These particular students are not making progress toward their goals. It looks like they are not going to make one year's progress. What barriers do you see? How can I help remove these barriers?	15. Was this student's progress what you expected based on your goal? How will this inform your instruction next year?
4. Predict the effect on this student's life if we were able to help him or her perform proficiently How can we work together to make that happen?	10. What conclusions have you drawn about how well this plan is working? What caused the progress? How will you replicate your successes with students?	16. At what level do you recommend this student begin next year? What are your recommendations to continue this student's "invisible excellence" (more than one year of progress in a single year) next year?
5. At the end of the year, what is your projected performance goal for this student?	11. How are you ensuring that students achieving on and above grade level are continuing to improve?	17. How do the data support your recommendations?
6. Some students need "invisible excellence"—more than one year's growth in a single year—to achieve grade-level standards. How much more progress, beyond one year, can this student make with you this year?	12. What additional data would help you understand this student's barriers to learning? How can I help you remove those barriers?	18. What professional development would support students' learning?

EXHIBIT 3.3 **Literacy Leadership Questioning for *District* Administrators**

Beginning of the Year	During the Year	End of the Year
A. Now it is your turn to hold the baton of school improvement! What measurable indicators of performance will be observed?	G. What impact has professional development had upon this system?	M. How much progress did each school make toward achieving its student performance goals?
B. Predict the effect your school improvement plan will have upon the performance of students. How can I support your efforts to make that happen?	H. Today, what would you do differently? How can I help you make this happen?	N. How did your reading or math level data support our district improvement goals?
C. What is the number of students performing on or above enrolled grade levels? How many students are performing more than one year below grade level in the academic core? How will you measure progress?	I. This particular school, grade, or team is not making progress toward its goals. It looks like this group is not going to achieve one year's progress. What barriers have you observed that impede progress? How can I help?	O. What do the summative data inform you about next year's school improvement goal?
D. What data do you need to gather? Who will be involved in the analysis? How will the conclusions be presented to the school and community? What groups are involved in developing the plan of action?	J. Predict each school's performance at the end of this year. What observable indicators informed your prediction? What are you doing to ensure your prediction becomes reality?	P. What subject subscales show significantly lower or higher results in this school/region than in others throughout this system?
E. How are literacy actions used to improve social studies, science, and math?	K. What conclusions were drawn from your data about how well your plan is working?	Q. At what level did your school/region/district perform on the state assessment? What progress do you predict will be made next year?
F. What achievement gaps have been identified and addressed between gender, ethnicity, socioeconomic status, and English Language Learner status?	L. What trends, strengths, and/or areas of concern did you identify in your school's common formative assessment data?	R. How did you determine which specific strategies directly impacted student achievement?

© The Leadership and Learning Center

Why is it, when change is needed in order to bring about improvement, that there is such difficulty implementing the change? At times, we get in our own way. We allow structures to become limiting factors, rather than discerning the entry level of change that can be effectively managed. Frequently, progress is prevented because there are no internal or external maps to guide our actions. We must have a visual representation of what it is we want to change and then locate the tools needed to make that change. The Disciplined Practice model concretely and visually depicts each phase of literacy leadership and the related literacy actions, as depicted in Exhibit 3.1.

Understanding (*explaining meaning; identifying how new initiatives improve performance*)

The literacy action of understanding focuses on the cycle of improvement by the leader and the participants. Compelling Conversations between and among leaders, participants, students, parents, and community members facilitate the emergence of understanding. Understanding occurs as leaders, participants, students, parents, and community members recognize their present reality and acknowledge their imminent future. During the igniting phase, issues frequently arise in the construction process of the improvement plans. Understanding brings balance between guiding and directing, as reflected in the following scenario.

Scenario for Understanding: Balancing Honesty and Enthusiasm

During a school improvement planning retreat, a new middle school principal was asked by the school improvement team chairperson, "Are funds available to do everything the team proposed in the school improvement plan to support literacy for the next school year?"

The principal responded, "Well, that is a great question; I need to think about whether funding is available in next year's budget to accomplish all of the goals."

Rather than giving the team an answer, the principal bought some time with his response. After the team meeting adjourned, I asked the principal why he delayed responding to the question about funding.

His response was, "I did not want to curb their enthusiasm. This was the first time since I became principal that the school improvement team was on board with me."

The principal's response to my question was not reassuring. Understanding was apparent, but it was incomplete without honesty.

The principal may have asked the school improvement chairperson, "Do you feel the plan has grown too large to be successfully implemented in a single school year?" creating an opportunity for the school improvement chairperson's opinion to be expressed. Through reflective questioning, the principal could have initiated an opportunity not only to hear the chairperson's thinking, but also to open the conversation to other members of the team.

Leaders in every situation find it difficult to remember that slower is often faster. Leaders want to lead, and to be recognized as capable of making decisions that participants acknowledge and celebrate. Leaders who dictate construction of the school improvement plan are perceived by participants as unresponsive and insensitive. Yet, unresponsive leaders are held responsible by participants for the plan and any ensuing failures. How do leaders implement a cycle of improvement without understanding the need for participant buy-in and support? They don't. Understanding the need for balancing decisions is a subtle, yet significant quality for success.

The igniting phase is a risk-free zone of investigation for participants. The successful launch of school and system cycles of improvement demands that participants acknowledge and accept ownership of their actions. When participants' actions do not produce the predicted results, leaders continue to support and recognize them for their commitment to the cycle of improvement.

Inferring (*basing decisions on connections within available information*)

Inferring requires the leader to draw vertical and horizontal connections between the data, instruction, and student progress at different grade levels. Leaders connect background information to generate commitment. They are able to guide without dictating, and generate an area of focus without appointing someone in charge of the initiative. Inferring will continue to become increasingly important as systems become more complex.

Guiding Questions to Support the Igniting Phase of Disciplined Practice

As a school leader, how will I:

- Ignite the spark leading to the adoption of the improvement plan?
- Determine what *new* questions will be posed to refine the school improvement process?
- Engage Data Teams in the igniting of improvement?
- Create/implement instruments which are nonevaluative but stress teacher and student accountability for changed instructional practice?

- Acknowledge effective practice and exemplary examples of teacher and student performance in my school?

- Draw out inferences from the data collected during professional development?

The next phase, the tending phase of Disciplined Practice, monitors and continues the progress from the igniting phase.

TENDING—PHASE 3 (MONITORING THE FLAME)

The tending phase of Disciplined Practice requires the leader to proceed with implementation of the adopted improvement plan. Tending is the process of monitoring the flame of fidelity required for the predicted improvement to occur. Fidelity of implementation is evaluated by data gathered through common formative assessments, walk-through observations, central office instructional rounds, Compelling Conversations, and Data Teams. The leader and participants schedule collaborative planning time to verify progress toward stated goals. The tending phase embraces the principles of Decision Making for Results: accountability, collaboration, and antecedents of success, while also celebrating success, identifying gaps as they arise, and realigning processes to meet or exceed stated goals. A fire requires tending in order to keep the flame alive. Improvement plans require tending to continue progress toward adopted goals.

Every intentional fire, no matter what the purpose for the flame, has a person responsible for monitoring it. This person may be at a grill, the designated chef for the day's cookout. This person assumes responsibility for stoking, spreading, and increasing or reducing the flame as needed. These actions are based on data. Fire tending requires conversations about how big the flame should become and how long the flame will exist. Side conversations occur when those "around the grill" share comments on how they like their food cooked. When I am the chef, my wife provides excellent feedback as she drops by to ensure that the outcome of every steak is not "Pittsburgh rare." These conversations provide feedback to the flame keeper, just as participants discuss data with leaders.

Fire tending has walk-through procedures to determine whether delivery is occurring, behaviors are observable, or habits are changing. Feedback is our friend, when wrapped in data. For example, someone may ask, "Do you think we need more wood on the fire? I'm feeling chilly" or someone may state, "I'm cold! Get more wood on the fire." Both types of feedback get results, but one permits the keeper of the flame to retain dignity. Respectful feedback influences outcomes.

> *Feedback is our friend, when wrapped in data.*

Once, when standing by the grill, I noticed my neighbor approaching with a big smile. The smell of my grilling had floated to his property. He checked out my spare ribs by eating one on the spot. He certified that the work was proceeding to plan, suggesting more sauce to improve the flavor, much like walk-throughs or instructional rounds enable the leader to assesses progress, rather than evaluate the product. Improvement plans in the tending phase require feedback that is not critical of the leader, plan, or participants, but is formative and specific. Transparent feedback based upon data respectfully presented is a powerful tool to energize individual, school, or system actions.

> *The infusion of accurate, timely data stokes the flame of improvement.*

In the tending phase, communication disconnects may occur. When communication breaks down, the leader assesses the problem and intervenes in the cycle of improvement to ensure communication flow is repaired. The leader's intervention, when it happens at the right time in the process, prevents the extinguishing of the cycle of improvement. The infusion of accurate, timely data stokes the flame of improvement. Leaders introduce data gathered from the monitoring process to energize participants and sustain commitment. Gaps in participant learning identified and acknowledged in the tending phase become a focus for job-embedded, just-in-time professional development designed and monitored to close gaps in participant knowledge.

The following questions and responses support leaders' thinking and decisions during the tending phase of Disciplined Practice.

- *How do literacy actions guide conversations that are honest and transparent?*
  Literacy actions provide the leader with a common vocabulary to communicate gaps in participant learning that hinder improvement of student performance. The leader and participant collaboratively determine interventions, create monitoring protocols, define assessment criteria, and set performance expectations.

- *Why does the leader progress-monitor students' performance?*
  Leaders and participants learn as a result of progress-monitoring student performance. Student performance and teacher accountability are opposite sides of a single coin. One cannot improve without increasing the capacity of the other. Teacher knowledge, skill, and talent support student growth, development, and motivation. Each reinforces the other's ability to grow and learn.

- *Why do leaders review, revise, and redirect the improvement process?*
  Leaders are charged with creating opportunities for participants and students

to learn. The improvement process is cyclical in practice and organic in nature. The organic nature of improvement demonstrates the evolving, emerging, and evolutionary character of the process. Literacy variables and interventions are modified continuously throughout the cycle. The leader must continually monitor to provide feedback to sustain students' momentum without permitting slippage into complacency. Leaders in the tending phase work on the cutting edge of change.

- *How does the leader know when to introduce and remove resources at the appropriate time?*
  Monitoring identifies "tipping points" (Gladwell, 2002), when the introduction or removal of resources would continue progressive momentum.

- *How does the leader introduce fresh data to flame actions?*
  Data is not hidden or disregarded out of fear that its introduction will cause a disturbance in the improvement process. The purpose for collecting data and introducing it into the improvement process is to correct misaligned practice, process, or product.

Leaders and teachers benefit equally when they are committed and eager to learn and to develop both personally and professionally in their craft. Literacy actions focused upon during the tending phase include *applying, exploring, judging,* and *monitoring.*

Applying (*implementing knowledge to achieve an outcome*)

Applying is a literacy action used during the tending phase of Disciplined Practice. The leader collaboratively resolves challenges and concerns participants raise as a result of the implementation of the improvement plan. It is during this phase that participants collaboratively close identified gaps in the improvement plan. The following scenario depicts an opportunity to resolve challenges through establishing meaningful connections.

Scenario for Applying: Identifying and Addressing Needs

Without the ability to make meaningful connections to the learning environment, success is not likely for teachers or their students. Not only do disconnects exist for students, there are broken lines of communication between district and school leaders who place teachers in environments without appropriate attention to the need to provide academic, intellectual, and cultural support for them. During a professional development session, one teacher asked me if I could provide a list of slang words for him so that he could better communicate with students. I found his request quite humorous: The teacher thought that because I was of the same ethnicity as many of the students, I would have a ready repertoire of slang words that I could share.

Recognizing his desire to improve, but lack of understanding about how to proceed, I offered to collaboratively model specific instructional techniques to support student learning. Literacy actions can be used as a framework for learning and as a tool for change to determine meaningful ways to establish relationships with students.

Evaluating (*appraising a situation, making a decision, and taking a stand*)

Evaluating is used by the leader to disaggregate formative data that was collected to compare student progress with predicted improvement goals. Evaluating in the tending phase ensures practice is aligned with the adopted goals. Evaluation focuses improvement and stimulates development of professional learning opportunities that are just-in-time, job-embedded, and data-driven. Evaluating formative monitoring data openly supports a culture of continuous improvement. Students' progress results are communicated to students, teachers, administrators, the superintendent, board members, and the community to enhance shared accountability. Evaluating demonstrates that improvement is about learning and not blaming. Lack of transparency in an educational organization limits opportunities to learn and improve from mistakes. Evaluating and openly presenting outcomes creates trust and builds commitment.

Exploring (*determining the nature of a problem and learning from your mistakes*)

During exploring, leaders frequently check participant feedback to determine components that are effective or ineffective with particular groups. Leaders bring teachers together to identify and adopt next steps and to glean insights from challenges that have been faced and addressed. New insights about challenges provide leaders and teachers alike with opportunities to realign actions. Leaders demonstrate exemplary leadership when they are able to clarify for all that the data is only information, not a personal affront or a reflection of one's work ethic. Exploring in the tending phase permits the leader and participants to make critical decisions about the project before participants lose commitment to the adopted goal and no longer believe the project has value or worth. It is possible for participants in the tending phase to disengage if they believe the value and worth of the improvement is not equal to their effort. Both choices doom the project and place the leader in the spotlight.

Judging (*slowing down to make a transparent decision based on evidence, while recognizing opinion*)

In Disciplined Practice, judging is when the leader determines the participants are not committed to continuing to work to achieve the goals. Judging requires determining what can be expected to be achieved if the same course of action is continued to completion.

Monitoring (*determining progress and addressing limiting factors*)

Monitoring is a literacy leadership action in the tending phase that district and school leaders use to determine how formative data acquired during the Decision Making for Results Process will nurture shared accountability among participants. Monitoring drives just-in-time decisions that inform practice. Monitoring provides the courageous leader an opportunity to modify lines of communication, clarify formative goals, and request assistance, as in the following scenario.

Scenario for Monitoring: Awareness Leads to Collaboration

During a site visit, a middle school principal voiced a concern about developing a master schedule which maximized instructional time and provided intervention opportunities within the school day. I asked, "Why do you believe your master schedule needs to be revised?"

The principal responded, "The intervention specialists in our building don't have time to adequately address student learning gaps."

I asked, "Do you believe the master schedule is the problem?"

The principal responded, "The master schedule was created before Response to Intervention (RTI) required tiered instruction and before common formative assessments. Also, the master schedule was developed before we had technology in place to provide intervention support for students."

I asked, "Did you discuss your concern with the leadership team?"

The principal responded, "The leadership team is aware and agreed the master schedule for the coming school year must be changed to create blocks of intervention time."

The principal admitted to having difficulty creating blocks of time within the master schedule and requested help. Collaboratively, a new master schedule was developed.

The tending phase of Disciplined Practice presents transparent opportunities for leaders to investigate issues they do not feel capable of addressing. Another tending phase scenario provides a look into the process of monitoring by a Data Team.

Scenario for Monitoring: Acting on Tipping Points

Tipping points, unique moments of opportunity to improve, if not acknowledged or handled appropriately by the leader, can result in the organization sliding into complacency (Gladwell, 2002, p. 259). This scenario provides a look into a team that took positive advantage of an opportunity to improve.

The fifth-grade team met to discuss the common formative mathematics assessment data from the second of the four annual benchmark assessments. The Data Team leader asked, "Why are more than half of our students failing to achieve mastery on this benchmark examination?" The team discussed the question and decided there were three gaps in mathematics skills prevalent among one-third of the students.

The Data Team leader asked, "What does our team need to know and be able to do to close this gap for our students?"

One of the members responded, "I am willing to take those students and work with them before school and over lunch on their math skills." The team leader asked, "Do we have other ideas?" A second member of the team offered to switch the ten lowest-performing students into her class, if twelve to fifteen of her students could be rescheduled into other teachers' classes for math instruction. Students were regrouped into other classes with parental approval.

Tipping points are wonderful opportunities to generate organizational excitement and propel participants to the next level of implementation. The action or inaction of the leader at the time of tipping point impacts initiatives and the potential success of the improvement. Tipping points can be as insignificant as requesting outside assistance to construct a master schedule or as detailed as regrouping students for math skills. The following guiding questions provide teachers with opportunities for reflective inquiry.

Guiding Questions to Support the Tending Phase of Disciplined Practice

The following guiding questions may be posed when formative data analysis indicates the actions taken (cause data) did not achieve predicted outcomes (effect data):

- What have been the effects of professional development on your instruction and the achievement of your students?

- How would you evaluate the impact of your disciplinary literacy lesson planning on the quality of your instruction? On student learning?

- How do you plan to share instructional models that have been successful for your students with other teachers?

The tending phase of Disciplined Practice relies on the banking phase to sustain progress.

BANKING—PHASE 4 (PRESERVING THE EMBERS)

The purpose of banking a fire is to preserve the spark contained within the burning embers, so that you can easily rekindle the fire the next day. The process of banking involves gathering the embers together in a pile and covering them with ash to reduce their contact with oxygen. Using ashes to cover the embers reduces the supply of oxygen available to the fire, thus preserving the spark by slowing down the consumption of fuel.

The banking of a school improvement initiative, much like the banking of a fire, occurs at the end of the improvement cycle, usually close to the end of the school year. The process of banking is critical to the continuation of the school's effort to build upon success. The purpose of banking in the school improvement cycle is to identify and preserve the acts of improvement that met or exceeded predicted outcomes and to discard the acts of improvement not producing the desired or predicted outcome.

Banking in the school improvement phase is the responsibility of the school leadership team. The school improvement team gathers formative data collected throughout the tending phase and summative reports from each of the subgroups implementing school improvement goals. The leadership team evaluates each component and identifies those achieving or exceeding predicted outcomes. These components, like the banking of a fire, will be placed together, supported, refined, analyzed, and refreshed for inclusion as a component of the next improvement plan. The data and reports gathered on components of the school improvement plan unable to achieve their predicted outcomes are analyzed by the team to determine the cause for their poor performance.

In the cycle of educational improvement, the baton of student progress is not dropped over summer vacations, between grade levels, or between different disciplines. The spark of learning remains buried within the embers of professional practice and teacher understanding, waiting to be rekindled the following school year by dynamic teachers and committed leadership teams. The banking phase of Disciplined Practice is associated with the literacy actions of *creating, evaluating, synthesizing,* and *understanding.*

The banking phase of Disciplined Practice captures best practices and retains procedural memory. Best practices are those instructional strategies and professional protocols used to address the individual needs and challenges of students performing below or beyond the normal predictable expectations of an average student. Procedural memories are structural and organizational processes embedded within the culture of the school which support interventions and opportunities for students performing outside predictable norms. The banking phase identifies and shares best practices between and among teachers, grade levels, and disciplines within the school and throughout the district. The banking phase of Disciplined Practice is critical to the success of the cycle of improvement. Banking, in Disciplined Practice, means gathering, sorting, preserving, and sharing information that provokes new ideas and acknowledges divergent points of view.

The following questions and responses clarify connections in the banking phase of Disciplined Practice:

- *What components of the cycle of improvement produced predicted results?*
  Adopting goals and predicting results is the mission of the cycle of improvement in organizations. The better the organization becomes at adopting goals and predicting results, the more closely aligned are practice, process, and product.

- *What impact on students, parents, and community members was observed?*
  The improvement plan, when fueled, ignited, tended, and banked openly and transparently, will have a positive impact upon stakeholder groups. The leader creates open lines of communication with the stakeholder community.

- *What future suggestions for improvement were identified in the banking phase?*
  The banking phase identifies suggestions for future improvements. Questions are posed and suggestions are made. This phase is needed in the cycle of improvement to explore and exhaust all possible avenues before presenting suggestions for future cycles of improvement.

- *What occurred that was successful, yet was not explicitly included in the school improvement plan?*
The banking phase identifies unexpected, unplanned, and unknown components that appear at the least opportune time. The banking phase is designed to identify and explain how this came to occur. It demands the rigorous literacy actions of *creating, evaluating, synthesizing,* and *understanding.*

Creating (*generating original points of view and products through innovative thoughts and patterns*)

Creating is the literacy action in the banking phase that leaders use while interpreting multiple summative data points and assessing the value added to the organization. During this phase, a determination is made about the value created by a combination of data-based inferences and ideas. This information provides support for future decisions. Creative leaders understand what is needed and also how to achieve predicted student outcomes. Today it is becoming vital for leaders to be creative with finances and initiatives to support school improvement as evidenced in student achievement.

Evaluating (*appraising a situation, making a decision, and taking a stand*)

Evaluating is the literacy action in the banking phase of Disciplined Practice that the leader and participants use to disaggregate data and glean summative findings. It is an open process the leader facilitates to stimulate participant input and acknowledge suggestions for investigations in the next cycle of improvement. Evaluating determines if adopted goals were achieved and provides the leader with the story behind the numbers by uncovering information. Evaluating is the reflective process that prepares the organization for the next cycle of improvement. It is important for the leader to acknowledge participation, as the following scenario depicts.

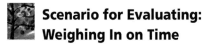 ## Scenario for Evaluating: Weighing In on Time

Our failure to achieve the results we are seeking can be attributed to our unwillingness to engage in the vital conversation needed to build relationships necessary for initiating and sustaining change in failing systems. If one never ventures into deep

> *If one never ventures into deep conversations about topics that support achievement, how would one ever know where options and opportunities for success lie?*

conversations about topics that support achievement, how would one ever know where options and opportunities for success lie? While collaborating in one school district in the southwest section of the country, I participated in a dialogue with a principal who expressed a desire to have more conversation with her teachers. She said, "It may be that regularly scheduled conversation will require more time than I have available."

My question to her was, "Available for what?" After a moment of silence, I explained, "When you weigh the value of the process of holding scheduled conversations, then evaluate the outcomes, the payoff, in terms of student progress, is much greater than the time spent."

Our conversation led to her beginning the process.

Synthesizing (*figuring out how different parts can become a whole*)

Synthesizing is the literacy action in the banking phase used by the leader and participants to produce a sequence of events for the purpose of identifying and describing gaps, overlaps, or breakdowns in the cycle of improvement.

Understanding (*explaining meaning generated from multiple data points and media*)

Understanding draws upon data to prepare informed opinions impacting the cycle of improvement. Understanding is employed in the new cycle of improvement to validate and ensure fidelity of practice and process.

Guiding Questions to Support the Banking Phase of Disciplined Practice

Leaders willing to question results in the banking phase of school improvement are not caught unprepared. The following questions initiate conversations about summative data. They must be followed with probing questions to determine the root causes of the data.

- What results were unexpected?

- What gaps in achievement identified future needs?

- What does the summative data reveal about the effectiveness of the school improvement effort?

- How does the synthesis of available data, and clarification of resulting questions, inform the creation of SMART goals for the future school improvement plan?

- What observable teacher behaviors and student actions will be included as walk-through literacy indicators uncovered in the banking phase of the previous cycle of improvement?

Chapter 3 Conclusion

Dear Readers,

I have come to the conclusion that having purpose establishes meaning in one's life. In this chapter, we have discussed how literacy actions establish meaningful connections for leadership in all four phases of Disciplined Practice. From fueling to igniting through tending and into banking, the embers of our personal commitment, desire to learn, professional curiosity, knowledge of craft, and belief in our ability to provide a world-class education for each and every student have not been extinguished. The spark resides within each of us and is glowing brightly, eagerly awaiting the removal of the ashes, the introduction of oxygen, the kindling to ignite the flame, and the fuel to create a conflagration that will hush naysayers and produce a thirst for learning in each and every child.

Sincerely,

Bill

CHAPTER 4

How Can Disciplinary Literacy Be Differentiated and Sustained?

> *It is no longer enough to have walked in the shoes of a leader, for those shoes were designed for jogs along 20th-century paths.*

With both of us having been principals and district leaders, we realize it is no longer enough to have walked in the shoes of a leader, for those shoes were designed for jogs along 20th-century paths. Although today's leaders must continue making collaborative decisions, not only is the brisk pace of decisions increasing, the leader's path itself is changing course while en route.

SUSTAINING LITERACY LEADERSHIP

Today's leaders require knowledge far beyond a synthesis of past experiences. No communication at all? Think about it: In a short length of time, the Common Core State Standards—with new curriculum and assessment components, the Elementary and Secondary Education Act, Race to the Top, the Partnership for 21st Century Skills, National Council for Teachers of English Frameworks, and new literacy research have all recently found their way to leaders' laptop screens. When have leaders experienced such a tsunami of far-reaching legislation and change initiatives? Compile these changes with a financial crisis of significant magnitude, along with "hundred-year" weather events impacting school calendars, and it is apparent how literacy actions are vital for leaders. When leadership includes the Disciplined Practice literacy leadership model described in Chapter 3, sustained change supports students' literacy progress. Of significance is the banking phase that sustains strengths, identifies failures, and carefully searches for hot pockets of potential that exist within the embers.

CONNECTING DISCIPLINED MINDS

While leaders are dealing with not just one, but a series of critical literacy dilemmas, adolescents have never before experienced such literacy independence. Forging ahead with gusto into the electronic world, *adolescents* are teaching adults the dance of the digital age. What about adolescents' lack of prior experience? The astounding design of adolescent brains, their plasticity when creating new connections, allows our adolescents to directly inform needed educational changes in the design of rigorous common standards and relevant instruction. With increasing access to unfiltered news, Google capabilities, and easily available digital information, and new increases in standards-based research expectations during school, receiving guidance about how to think and communicate like a citizen journalist is vital for adolescents. Savvy technological skills, unbounded by the literacy actions in Chapter 1, or untethered by Habits of Mind, can have unfathomable results. If leaders do not embrace the urgent responsibility to guide adolescents in acquiring the attributes of a Disciplined Mind (Gardner, 2008, p. 21), learners will continue to seek information as an end in itself, rather than achieving their "human capacity to transform information into knowledge" (Hyerle, 2009, p. 13).

> *Adolescents are teaching adults the dance of the digital age.*

TRANSFERRING DISCIPLINARY LITERACY INSTRUCTION

Disciplinary Literacy research is providing findings that dispute the generalized "reading in the content areas" strategies and enhancing them by focusing on the unique literacy needs within each discipline. Connections with being a citizen journalist engage students in deeper understanding as they apply literacy actions and Habits of Mind. Hattie acknowledges the need for a major shift away from surface information to a balance of surface and deep learning that leads to students being able to construct understanding (2009, pp. 28–29). Surface learning, deep processes, and constructed understanding directly exemplify the comprehension outcomes provided by the Disciplinary Literacy four-stage instructional model described in Chapters 1 and 2. When a subject area is reframed as a "discipline" rather than a "content," the intended learning outcomes shift from being a list of findings to being patterns of behavior for "doing the work of the subject properly" (Wiggins and McTighe, 2007, p. 47) to avoid misunderstandings. The need to think and act as "transfer abilities" (p. 48) within *each discipline* is different than learning factual content and skills. Reconceiving content areas as disciplines requires that "every subject area … be framed around … a set of worthy and diverse performances that concretely represent long-term, desired accomplishment—the *discipline* of doing all subjects well" (p. 48). Senge's seminal *The Fifth Discipline* correlates with Wiggins and McTighe by stating, "To practice a discipline is to be a lifelong learner" (1990, p. 11). More than two decades later, reading research is disclosing evidence that concurs.

Explicit Disciplinary Literacy instruction that provides adolescents with graphic

> As communication by students merges with the attributes of becoming adolescent citizen journalists, literacy themes resound with Habits of Mind.

filters for guiding questions to focus on accuracy and understanding, together with explicit instruction on literacy actions and Habits of Mind, guide deep reading for all students. As communication by students merges with the attributes of becoming adolescent citizen journalists, literacy themes resound with Habits of Mind. Exhibit 4.1 connects emerging behaviors of adolescent citizen journalists with Habits of Mind to enhance understanding in each discipline and life.

With career and college standards integrated into the K–12 English Language Arts Common Core State Standards expecting student research to use digital resources, adolescent and intermediate students are expected to demonstrate active communication roles. Acquiring and analyzing information, then disseminating accurate, reliable knowledge as a responsible citizen, requires explicit instruction of literacy actions and Habits of Mind. All students and adults benefit from increasing their use of Habits of Mind.

Confronted with continuous distractions, can our "click-it and git-it" culture potentially impair the brain's ability to focus on "deep reading" (Wolf and Barzillai, 2009)? As Superintendent Barbara Whitecotton explained, "It is one thing to consider the role of adolescent citizen journalists. When recognizing the potential for manipulation and universal change, it becomes frightening to consider the global society we may be leaving for our kids. If we do not recognize the significance of developing our kids' literacy capacities to think as citizen journalists on a daily basis, there may be no future as we know it" (2010).

The benefit of expanding and sustaining connections between disciplines is that it increases connections between levels of elementary, middle, and high school that will promote student progress. Recently, while walking in these district-level comfortable-*looking* shoes, I visited a high school where students remembered me as their principal. Our hallway conversation included stories about making the football team and their latest tattoos. Later, while doing a walk-through in a ninth-grade reading class designed to support struggling students, the students' greetings shifted: hoods went up, eyes glanced down. These students ... *my* students ... appeared uncomfortable about me finding out that they were in *this* class. Truly, I was the one feeling saddened, wondering if there was anything we could have done differently to support these students. I questioned myself and others: "How does this happen? Why don't principals and school leaders know students' progress *after* they leave their school?" When our students moved on to middle schools and high schools, I believed *every one* of them would be successful, that progress would continue, and

EXHIBIT 4.1

Connecting Habits of Mind with Adolescent Citizen Journalist Behaviors to Guide Deep Reading for all Disciplines

Managing Impulsivity	Consider the impact on others when making decisions and communicating in person or electronically.
Thinking and Communicating with Clarity and Precision	Be a credible person by being honest with yourself about your own perceptions and biases. Be aware of your potential to have a positive global impact.
Thinking Flexibly	Be open about problems and address issues from new angles as different data is received.
Striving for Accuracy	Take time to be a responsible and reliable person by checking for correct information prior to sending electronic messages.
Questioning and Posing Problems	Fill the space between what you know and what you do not know with smart questions.
Taking Responsible Risks	Recognize that all risks are not worth taking when trying to go beyond limits.
Thinking about Thinking (Metacognition)	Explore further by thinking about your thinking. Form questions in search of accurate, meaningful information.
Applying Past Knowledge to New Situations	Pull out meaning from one source or experience and apply it in a different situation.
Gathering Data through All Senses	Gather specific data from many different sources to make the information accurate.
Creating, Imagining, Innovating	Develop solutions to new problems and find ways to improve current life situations for yourself and others.
Thinking Interdependently	Think collaboratively and talk with others about an idea or problem.

Habits of Mind in this chart are from Costa and Kallick (2008) that eventually the underachieving students would make it. In some cases, I was wrong. Yet, I would not have known if it were not for the fact that I now had a pre-K–12 leadership viewpoint to establish district connections between levels. Accurate, regularly scheduled communication about all students is an easy preventative action for districts. Regie Routman (2010) explained how educators who encouraged, supported, and remained in contact with a group of young English Language Learner students provided these students with a path for achieving their dreams. Student progress through middle and high school must be communicated to elementary levels to inform instructional decisions from the beginning. This alignment is a significant potential outcome from the aligned Common Core State Standards that will benefit struggling learners and all students.

ENGAGING ENGLISH LANGUAGE LEARNERS AND STRUGGLING LEARNERS

Coinciding with the Common Core State Standards is research that depicts the need to distribute leverage for literacy within each discipline; much like rotating gears need to mesh to work in tandem.

Disconnected disciplines, different levels of school, and unaligned national and state expectations for each level have taken their toll on all our students' progress. Presently, concrete changes have begun, with national and state organizations supporting alignment of rigorous standards. Coinciding with the Common Core State Standards is research that depicts the need to distribute leverage for literacy *within* each discipline; much like rotating gears need to mesh to work in tandem. Specific Disciplinary Literacy instruction for each discipline focuses explicit instruction on comprehension specific to that content area. All the while, literacy actions and Habits of Mind prevent slippage of rigor and provide strong connections by creating paths of action.

Instruction that honors comprehension in each discipline needs to be differentiated to meet the needs of all students, especially for English Language Learners. Linda Gregg provides the core principles for Response to Intervention and explicit strategies for the three tiers of intervention in *Power Strategies for Response to Intervention*. She explains, "Rather than waiting for a general education student to fail or be referred to special education, schools now require interventions and assessments that meet the individual needs of all students" (2010, p. 9). Tier I instruction for all students includes research-based curriculum and instruction, heterogeneous and homogenous grouping, and instruction provided by the general education teacher within the regular classroom, where 80–85 percent of all students should be demonstrating progress (Gregg, 2010, p. 21).

Mastering concepts in the disciplines of history, science, English, mathematics, and music can be challenging. As the examples provided in Chapter 2 reflect, students struggling with comprehension will benefit from explicit Disciplinary Literacy instruction because inherent in this process is improvement of comprehension skills. Exhibit 4.2 explains how Disciplinary Literacy instruction provides Tier 1 opportunities for struggling learners to be successful.

Required to view information from polished textbooks, students have had only nominal direct connections with discipline-based raw material. This has resulted in minimal demand on adolescents' literacy skills, engagement in reading, and motivation to transfer information into knowledge for other disciplines or life situations. Combined with this fact is that by the time students are adolescents, it is likely that they have had explicit instruction on general "reading in the content areas" comprehension strategies within the basic and intermediate comprehension levels taught at elementary and middle school grades, and that's about all. Disciplinary Literacy provides the skills that adolescents from previous eras learned over time, as they gradually grew into adulthood. Such skills were typically not taught explicitly, but acquired through experience. This gift of time is gone—replaced by decisions made in the moment by adolescents. Habits of Mind and literacy actions focus on behaviors that not only prevent slippage for each discipline but that transmit to life situations.

THREE ELEMENTS FOR DISCIPLINARY LITERACY INSTRUCTION

Differentiating classroom Disciplinary Literacy instruction includes focusing on three elements: *content*—what or how the student needs to learn, *process*—activities for engaging learning, and *products*—demonstrating understanding (Gregg, 2010, p. 79). Disciplinary Literacy instruction integrates components of each of the three elements. Chapters 1 and 2 include recommendations for specifically identified vocabulary and discipline-based comprehension questions that are "student-friendly" (Breiseth, 2010).

Content

Disciplinary Literacy differentiation opportunities are directly integrated into the instructional process to increase teacher options for providing Tier I comprehension instruction. Disciplinary Literacy differentiation can be achieved through the following recommendations:

- Select reading materials from different text complexity levels.
- Integrate the students' background knowledge to build connections between their experience and discipline-based information.

EXHIBIT 4.2 **Tier 1 Disciplinary Literacy Instruction for English Language Learners and Struggling Learners**

1. The engagement of critical thinking in literacy actions is motivational as English Language Learners are able to apply their strengths in thinking to reading with increased understanding at the interpretative levels. Explicit instruction on literacy actions (see pages 26–59) leads to English Language Learners and struggling learners identifying important points in the text and being able to complete related assignments. Student-friendly definitions are included for each Literacy Action to differentiate the process.

2. Providing comprehension instruction to teach students to read like historians shifts their purpose from learning only facts. Engaging conversations about the author's motive provide insight beyond the details, events, and dates, translating information into knowledge. When students understand *motive,* they are able to transfer it to other disciplines and to life. Similar comparisons hold true for the disciplines of science, English, and math. Student-friendly text investigation questions are bolded for each stage and discipline to differentiate the process and product.

3. Habits of Mind and literacy actions prevent slippage as different disciplines engage, enhancing struggling students' understanding of the big picture—the core discipline. These connections access the strengths of struggling learners' critical thinking.

4. The interactions resulting from deep understanding throughout multiple disciplines impacts the quality of students' real-life communication as citizen journalists.

5. The Disciplinary Literacy model accepts that students are not referencing hard copies of encyclopedias and dictionaries, but acquiring references online. Technology is the fabric of adolescent citizen journalists' lives. Skills struggling students acquire through honoring each discipline first, then transmitting knowledge, will produce an advantage for all adolescents and for the emerging citizen journalist culture.

- Preview the text to focus on how the text features and organizational structures enhance comprehension.
- Use the Disciplinary Literacy filters to build comprehension through inquiry.
- Provide key vocabulary in original and student-friendly definitions. For example, each of the vocabulary terms listed as literacy actions in Chapter 1 include student-friendly versions.
- Offer students support for understanding connecting words and hedges, such as "perhaps," "maybe," and "because."
- Provide practice using literacy actions such as *evaluating* and *inferring*.
- Actively engage struggling students with words by using real-life stories and related questions (as described with each literacy action in Chapter 1).
- Check on comprehension by monitoring responses to the bold, student-friendly focus questions included in each section of the Disciplinary Literacy filters in Chapter 2.
- Monitor student progress with literal questions from the text stage of each discipline in Chapter 2.
- Monitor student progress using the interpretative questions from the subtext stages in Chapter 2.
- Monitor student progress with transfer questions from the citizen journalist questions in Chapter 1.
- Be certain to include critical thinking questions requiring all students to incorporate literacy actions, such as synthesizing and analyzing to ascertain actual comprehension.
- Incorporate the graphics available in digital or paper format for each Disciplinary Literacy filter. This will access students' thinking without requiring extensive directions.
- Ask English Language Learners and struggling students to demonstrate their comprehension through summarizing important points and incorporating key vocabulary.
- The Disciplinary Literacy Four-Stage Text Investigation instructional models are provided in text formats, visual graphics/nonlinear representations, and active versions that come alive on electronic devices. (www.leadandlearn.com)
- Provide small-group instruction for reteaching or extending learning.

Process

It is important to note that differentiating Disciplinary Literacy instruction must not diminish the depth of thinking expected of students. The purpose for providing tiered instruction is to modify the means of learning, not limit the use of strengths within students' knowledge, their literacy actions, or their Habits of Mind. With one advantage of Disciplinary Literacy being the high level of engagement, due to students' critical thinking accessed through "text investigating," it is vital to maintain the high level of thinking inherent in Disciplinary Literacy while modifying the process to access it as described in the following suggestions:

- Make options available to English Language Learners and struggling students, such as completing only the focus questions on each Disciplinary Literacy filter (the questions in bold) to adjust the length of the assignment.

- Provide students with digital access to the Disciplinary Literacy filters for acquiring comprehension of information.

- Extend the length of time for completing assignments to support English Language Learners and struggling learners. Engage advanced learners by extending collaborative research opportunities for deeper understanding about related topics *they* want to explore.

Products

Disciplinary Literacy products can be differentiated by providing options for students to complete individual or group products.

- Products can be independently or collaboratively completed.

- Understandings can be provided digitally on the electronic graphics, with pencil and paper using the handouts in Chapters 1 and 2, or through electronic communication.

Additionally, differentiating the adolescent learning environment for Disciplinary Literacy is easily accomplished by checking in with students about their preferences. It can include providing quiet places that limit distractions, offering locations for collaborative conversations about text investigation questions, providing options for students to move around while learning, and helping students to develop both tolerance and respect for other students' learning styles.

Thinking and communicating like a historian, scientist, mathematician, literary critic, musician, and citizen journalist provides an authentic, transferable synthesis of information *and* a significant depth of understanding for all students, including English Language Learners and struggling learners. For example, reading like a mathematician helps struggling students and all adolescents experience why and how reading closely, slowly, and focusing on visuals such as mathematical graphs improves comprehension. Therefore, process skills that are beneficial for following directions in careers are improved. Reading like a historian develops awareness and understanding about author bias—a real-world necessity for 21st-century communicators. Reading like a musician provides experience with abstract thinking. Specific connections between different disciplines are most evident in music.

The natural motivation inherent in the concept of Disciplinary Literacy reflects authentic understanding that respects the content in each discipline and the thinking of every student. Combined with solid, life-transferable Disciplinary Literacy actions and life-enhancing Habits of Mind, literacy exceeds previous isolated, skill-based standards that students think are devoid of meaningful purpose. The research-based constructs aligned with literacy leadership offer direction and motivation to increase the pace of literacy progress as measured by student achievement in each discipline, internationally benchmarked standards, and relevance with adolescents' lives as reliable citizen journalist communicators in the global network.

Chapter 4 Conclusion

Dear Readers,

The conclusion for this chapter is actually a beginning. Disciplinary Literacy is prying open a portal of understanding about deep connections. Both within each discipline and among different disciplines, understanding is explicit when all students are engaged in thinking and learning. When literacy actions become second nature, and Habits of Mind guide decisions, students are able to apply their critical thinking without slipping between the invisible cracks created by transitions between schools and levels. Providing instruction that honors the unique literacy qualities of the different disciplines, and respects adolescents' natural expertise and motivation with technology, will create paths of action that benefit each student.

Sincerely,

Thommie

Conclusions

W hy is it that many art museums have red velvet rope barriers preventing you from stepping in for a closer look? Would being able to see the actual brushstrokes limit your engagement with the artwork? Let's find out.

What can you notice in the closer view that was not apparent from the general, distant view (as when using "reading in the content area" strategies)?

A close focus on each separate poppy allows it to be considered in depth, while observing how the integration of many different colors enhances the larger perspective, just as Disciplinary Literacy provides focus and deeper understanding for each discipline.

During a Leadership and Learning Center retreat, we were invited to an evening of painting. An enthusiastic artist provided instruction that was not generalized—we did not all gather together and paint one large picture. Rather, her instruction was *distributed* to enhance our art literacy by providing specifics about how different brushes provide unique qualities, and which colors blend to provide interesting results. We incorporated this new information, along with our personal knowledge, to paint separate canvases, providing a memorable self-determining experience. Although the larger and distant view of the painting provides one perspective, the closer view reveals relevant details that comprise the end result. This is what happens when a student questions emotional truth while reading like a literary critic.

As curators of students' K–16 progress for the 21st century, we need to lift the red velvet barrier that has prevented us from stepping inside student progress for a close inspection, in conjunction with student data, to the instructional decisions that lead to truly masterpiece results. Expertise in developing common formative assessments, along with participating in Data Teams, have provided insight about vital changes needed in instructional decisions *before* the end of the marking period. On the other side of the coin, recent research in Disciplinary Literacy instruction is disclosing significant findings about what we sensed to be true: "reading in the content areas" strategies have not sufficiently provided the rigorous literacy instruction needed to prepare adolescents for the challenges of reading sophisticated, disciplined-based textbooks, frequently having lexiles years above a student's enrolled grade level.

Just as curators remain attuned to details to determine provisions for the interpretation and communication of each collection, we must honor the unique literacy qualities and demands of each discipline when providing instruction. By raising the red velvet rope barrier and stepping inside for a closer look at the important differences between reading like a historian, reading like a scientist, reading like a literary critic, reading like a mathematician, and reading like a musician, specific instruction can be provided to release *all* students' potential for deeper understanding.

Yet, engaging students with explicit instruction for *specific* disciplines does not eliminate the need for establishing connections among *all* disciplines. Through explicit instruction of literacy actions in all disciplines, students can acquire deep understanding applicable to different disciplines and to life.

Why are these increased responsibilities for all educators important? Today, our responsibilities as curators of students' literacy progress include literacy leadership to establish and model literacy expectations. We are also responsible for preparing students to question unfiltered information and communicate responsibly as adolescent citizen journalists, just as the Times Square terrorist bombing attempt in May 2010 was reported by two street vendors simply taking a closer look, which should remind us of our collective responsibility.

It is our hope that stepping inside for a closer look at adolescent Disciplinary Literacy will provide direction for student achievement and life decisions. Once inside, we believe it will be difficult to remain satisfied with the distant, generalist perspective.

Not waiting for adulthood any longer, decisions once sequestered from the purview of adolescents now intrude into their fragile reality. Face-to-face with life-altering choices that may threaten their futures, adolescents must employ Habits of Mind with literacy actions for all communication as they access digital media for school and pleasure. They are adolescent citizen journalists leading self-determining lives. Can we delay literacy's progress until we, as adult educators, are comfortable with the changes?

Take a look around.

Are our adolescents waiting?

Glossary

21st-Century Literacy—The dynamic interaction of exploring disciplines, creating understanding, and communicating knowledge, prompting explosive technological and societal changes.

Adolescent Literacy—The range of communication practices engaged in by students from grades 4 to 12.

Aesthetics—How a discipline satisfies the human predilection for artistic appreciation.

Applying—Implementing knowledge to achieve an outcome by connecting, synthesizing, and understanding.

Banking—The concluding phase of Disciplined Practice, when it is determined which processes improved student achievement.

Basic Literacy—Literacy skills such as decoding and knowledge of high-frequency words that underlie virtually all reading tasks (Shanahan and Shanahan, 2008).

Beliefs—The basis on which a reader can connect to other people or characters and understand why they act as they do.

Butterfly Effect—Very small changes in initial conditions resulting in wide, unexpected outcomes.

Chaos Theory—In literacy, occurs at the intersection of the attributes that explain the significance of the connections between the abstract theory and the concrete direction. It occurs on the edge of learning.

Civics—The application of knowledge gleaned from society and historical study to infer possible individual consequences.

Compelling Conversations—Conversations between students and teachers, administrators and teachers, and central office staff and board of education members that are accountable and improve student progress.

Conflict—Opposing actions and interests that can precipitate, impact, shape, and alter deeply ingrained beliefs in characters and readers.

Connection—In literacy, the association or relationship experienced by a reader who can follow the actions, experiences, and challenges of characters, both real and imagined, through their daily lives in the text.

Content Literacy—Teachers "show students how to use the reading and writing strategies needed to construct content knowledge" (Vacca and Vacca, 1999).

Context—The joining of the meaning of the words used in a text with the underlying meaning provided by understanding the origins of the text.

Continuous Pressure—In Chaos Theory, a process that shapes chaotic behaviors.

Conventional Literacy—Mastery of the standard instrument of knowledge and communication (Hirsch, 1988).

Creating—Generating something new, sometimes by combining familiar components in a new way.

Cycle of Improvement—Refers to improvement models that include the stages "plan, do, study, act."

Data Teams—Small grade-level or department teams that examine individual student work generated from common formative assessments; Data Team members attend collaborative, structured, scheduled meetings that focus on the effectiveness of teaching and learning (Besser, Anderson-Davis, and Peery, 2006).

Deep Understanding—Comprehension that honors each discipline and is transferrable to different disciplines and to life.

Depth of Understanding—Emerges from skill, strategy, process, and the application of literacy actions to complex or unique situations, forming meaning and ultimately creating knowledge.

Disciplinary Literacy—Literacy skills specialized to history, science, mathematics, literature, or some other subject (Shanahan and Shanahan, 2008).

Disciplined Mind—Learners who have a Disciplined Mind "see information not as an end in itself, but to think in ways that characterize the major disciplines ... science, mathematics, and history, and at least one art form" (Gladwell, 2010).

Disciplined Practice—A leadership approach to change that establishes direct connections between the work of leaders, actions of teachers, and achievement of students. It is a leadership model for leaders to personally own and use literacy actions for guiding teachers and students, rather than outsourcing literacy to professional developers for guiding teachers.

Emotional Truth—The answer to the question, "What do my feelings about the text tell me about myself that I did not realize before?"

Empathy—The reader's ability to identify with and understand another's situation, feelings, and motives.

Evaluating—Appraising a situation, making a decision, and taking a stand.

Exploring—Determining the nature of a problem and learning from your mistakes.

Filters—In the context of Disciplinary Literacy, filters allow readers to input knowledge, transform it in different ways, and produce evidence of that transformation that reflects learning.

Fractal—In Chaos Theory, a simple repetition of detail but in a smaller, descending scale.

Fueling—The beginning phase of Disciplined Practice, during which the critical need is identified and a "viral story" is created.

Guiding Questions—Questions designed to facilitate new knowledge, create learning, and present new ideas.

History—A discipline that allows one to understand, manage, and shape meaning in their world.

Homeostasis—The theory that a system or school will maintain its environment even when its function or condition has been disrupted.

Igniting Phase—The second phase of Disciplined Practice, during which SMART goals are created and a plan of action based upon the goals is developed. The leader and school improvement team enroll participants and begin the cycle of improvement during this phase.

Impersonal Subtext—The information "between the lines" of a text that allows the reader to deduce the plan and purpose of the author.

Inferring—Basing a decision on connections within available information.

Intellectual Connectedness—Thoughts sharing related features that can shape ideas and impact decisions.

Intentions—What the author of a text meant to convey by writing it.

Intermediate Literacy—Literacy skills common to many tasks, including generic comprehension strategies, common word meanings, and basic fluency (Shanahan and Shanahan, 2008).

Iteration—In Chaos Theory, the process through which multiple fractals, or details, are created on an increasingly smaller scale.

Judging—Slowing down to make a transparent decision based on evidence, while recognizing opinion.

Key Person—The protagonist readers compare and contrast themselves with.

Literacy Action Frameworks—The frame within which all one's literacy actions occur. The framework supports one's capacity to integrate information for meaning, form questions, and develop patterns of understanding. The framework provides a clear focus for establishing connections to promote consistent behavioral transfer, thus facilitating learning.

Literacy Actions (Analyzing, Applying, Creating, Evaluating, Exploring, Inferring, Judging, Monitoring, Questioning, Synthesizing, Understanding)—Literacy Actions are continuously evolving and are incorporated within the motion of learning, leadership, and life connections.

Literature—Text that arouses emotion by presenting the experience of human societies through the lives of characters and condensing the human experience.

Message—What the author intends to communicate to the reader by driving the key elements of the text.

Monitoring—Determining progress and addressing limiting factors.

Motive—The reason for a person's desire to act; the meaning beneath the text that reveals the author's reason for writing it.

Original Environment—The time, place, and circumstances in which the author places the reader, and the prior knowledge the reader possesses before reading the text.

Path of Action—The connection of two or more disciplines that creates an advantage in learning and leading. The correct next step on the journey to the achievement of one's goal.

Personal Subtext—The meaning that a reader gets out of a text that is particular to that reader's personal circumstances.

Process Learning—The highest form of learning and the most appropriate base for curriculum change and employing knowledge not merely as a composite of information but as a system for continuous learning (Hyerle, 2009).

Progress Monitor—To review the course of action and present a reminder when the system or school does not move toward the adopted or stated goal.

Questioning—Leading to appropriate decisions and solving problems effectively through reflective practice by expressing doubt, examining, probing, interrogating, querying, and inquiring.

Readers—Humans who connect with a text by personalizing and owning it to a deeper level, thus changing their thinking and ultimately their lives.

Reflective Practice—Questioning one's own practices and how they arrived at the actions taken.

Situation—The conflicts and events in a person's life that ultimately shape that person's beliefs; where an author or key person is "coming from."

Skills—"Highly generalizable basic skills that are entailed in all or most reading tasks." Includes "recognition of high-frequency words, and some basic fluency routines" (Shanahan and Shanahan, 2008).

Strategies—Multi-steps that support "cognitive endurance to maintain attention to more extended discourse, to monitor their own comprehension, and use various fix-up procedures if comprehension is not occurring" (Shanahan and Shanahan, 2008).

Student-Friendly Terms—Terms a student from fourth grade through adulthood can apply to differentiate and uncover knowledge.

Student Performance—The degree to which students demonstrate knowledge.

Subtext—The information hidden in a text that reveals the author's purpose, plan, motives, and intentions for writing the text.

Synthesizing—Produces a sequence of events for the purpose of identifying and describing gaps, overlaps, or breakdowns in the cycle of improvement.

Teacher Accountability—The state of being responsible, answerable, and liable for the learning of students.

Tending—The third phase of Disciplined Practice, during which formative achievement results providing focused, open, honest, truthful, and transparent data used to identify gaps in process, product, or practice at every level are generated.

Text—The fabric communicated to the reader that results from a writer weaving thoughts and intentions together.

Text Comprehension—A level of understanding that reaches beyond words and phrases to embrace intention, motive, purpose, and plan, the same concepts humans use to decipher the actions of others.

Thinking Maps—Graphic organizers that help educators provide fundamental cognitive skills for fluidly constructing knowledge to improve literacy for all disciplines and for leadership.

Thought Experiment—A thinking activity in which students design a scientific experiment on paper that, if conducted, could yield observable data that could be applied to answer the scientific question or resolve the dilemma chosen by them.

Tipping Points—In education, opportunities to generate organizational excitement and propel participants to the next level of implementation.

Understanding—The ability to explain meaning; the ability to identify how new initiatives improve performance.

Viral Story—The description leaders create to promote an urgent need critical to the improvement of student learning and lives. The viral story provides credence, generates support, and ensures participant commitment because it connects with a deep sense of purpose that is within us, waiting to be released.

Vision—The Disciplinary Literacy vision is that learners and leaders will be able to apply dynamic literacy actions and Habits of Mind using the Disciplinary Literacy inquiry model to be smart consumers and communicators of multimedia information during their evolving academic and personal lives.

Walk-Through—A structured procedure used in schools to determine if observable change is evident that validates the implementation of professional development or school improvement goals.

References

Adler, L. G., & Adler, S. J. (1999). *Letters of the century: America 1900–1999*. New York: The Dial Press/Random House.

Ainsworth, L., & Viegut, D. (2006). *Common formative assessments: How to connect standards-based instruction and assessment*. Thousand Oaks, CA: Corwin Press.

Alexander, A. (2009, March 8). Catch 'em while they're young. *The Washington Post*. Retrieved from http://www.washingtonpost.com/wp-dyn/content/article/2009/03/06/AR2009030602433_2.html?sid=ST2009031302712

Almeida, L., & Ainsworth, L. (2009). *Engaging classroom assessments: The making standards work certification course series*. Seminar by The Leadership and Learning Center, Englewood, CO.

Alvermann, D. E. (2009). Reaching/teaching adolescents: Literacies with a history. In J. V. Hoffman and Y. Goodman (Eds.), *Changing literacies for changing times: An historical perspective on the future of reading research public policy, and classroom practices* (pp. 98–107). New York: Routledge.

American Institutes for Research. (2005). Highlights from the 2003 New York State assessment of adult literacy. Albany, NY: National Assessment of Adult Literacy. p. 6.

Anderson, G. L., & Grinberg, J. (1998). Educational administration as a disciplinary practice: Appropriating Foucault's view of power, discourse, and method. *Educational Administration Quarterly, 34*(3), 329–353.

Anderson, L. W., & Krathwohl, D. R. (2000). *A taxonomy for learning, teaching, and assessing: A revision of Bloom's taxonomy of educational objectives*. Needham Heights, MA: Allyn & Bacon.

Bauer, S. W. (2003). *A well-educated mind*. New York: W.W. Norton and Company.

Besser, L., Almeida, L., Anderson-Davis, D. M., Flach, T., Kamm, C., & White, S. (2008). *Decision making for results: Data-driven decision making*. 3rd ed. Englewood, CO: Lead + Learn Press.

Besser, L., Anderson-Davis, D. M., & Peery, A. (2006). *Data teams*. Englewood, CO: Center for Performance Assessment.

Bloom, B. (1956). *Taxonomy of educational objectives: The classification of educational goals. Handbook 1: Cognitive domain*. White Plains, NY: Longman.

Brain Technologies. (2009). The brain: visual information management. Visual Thesaurus. Retrieved from www.thebrain.com/?gclid=CLLum8fzoKECFZdL5QodFFROww

Breiseth, L. (2010, March 3). Reading comprehension strategies for English Language Learners. *ASCD Express*. Retrieved from www.ascd.org/ascd_express/vol5/511_breiseth.aspx

Briggs, J., & Peat, F. D. (1990). *Turbulent mirror: An illustrated guide to chaos theory and the science of wholeness.* New York: HarperCollins.

Brummitt, C. (2010, April 18). Foiled Taliban attack using boy, 14, detailed: Suspect says he made suicide vests for Pakistan extremists. Retrieved from http://www.msnbc.msn.com/id/36630192/ns/world_news-south_and_central_asia/

Carnegie Corporation. (2010). *Time to act: An agenda for advancing adolescent literacy for college and career success.* New York. pp. 13–19 and 79.

Cassidy, J., Valadez, C. M., Garrett, S. D., & Barrera, E. S. (2010, March). Adolescent and adult literacy: What's hot, what's not. *Journal of Adolescent and Adult Literacy.* International Reading Association. Retrieved from www.reading.org/Publish.aspx?page=JAAL-53-6-Cassidy.html&mode=retrieve&D=10.1598/JAAL.53.6.1&F=JAAL-53-6-Cassidy.html&key=6DC9C417-B967-4403-B261-F3ED825E697B

Churches, A. (2009, January 4). Bloom's digital taxonomy: It's not about the tools, it's using the tools to facilitate learning. Retrieved from http://edorigami.wikispaces.com/Bloom's+Digital+Taxonomy

City, E. A., Elmore, R. F., Fiarman, S. E., & Teitel, L. (2009). *Instructional rounds in education: A network approach to improving teaching and learning.* Cambridge, MA: Harvard Education Press. p. 168.

Coiro, J., Knobel, M., Lankshear, C., & Leu, D. J. (2008). *The handbook of research on new literacies.* Mahwaw, NJ: Erlbaum.

Combley, R., Murphy, M., Rammell, C., Wedgeworth, L., & Watson, J. (Eds.). (2005). *Collins cobuild student's dictionary, plus grammar.* Glasgow, Great Britain: HarperCollins.

Common Core State Standards Initiative. (2010, June 10). Common core state standards for English language arts & literacy in history/social studies, science, and technical subjects. Washington, DC: Council of Chief State School Officers and the National Governors Association. Retrieved from www.corestandards.org

Costa, A. and Kallick, B. (2000a). *Activating & engaging habits of mind.* Alexandria, VA: Association for Supervision and Curriculum Development.

Costa, A., & Kallick, B. (2000b). *Integrating & sustaining habits of mind.* Alexandria, VA: Association for Supervision and Curriculum Development.

Costa, A., & Kallick, B. (2008). *Learning and leading with habits of mind: 16 essential characteristics for success.* Alexandria, VA: Association for Supervision and Curriculum Development. pp. 59–68.

Daragahi, B. (2009, July 5). Former Iran PM remains unbowed. *The Washington Post,* p. A5.

Darling-Hammond, L. (2010). *The flat world and education: How America's commitment to equity will determine our future.* New York: Teachers College Press. p. 7.

Dennis, B. (2009, December 30). E-mail inside AIG reveals executives struggling with growing crisis. *The Washington Post*. Retrieved from http://www.washingtonpost.com/wp-dyn/content/article/2009/12/29/AR2009122903322.html

Dessauer, C. (2008, December 11). Campaign politics and the Internet. C-Span Video Library, Forum 12/11/08, one hour and 31 minutes. Retrieved from http://www.c-spanvideo.org/program/282756-1

Devlin, K. (2008, March). Lockhart's Lament. Mathematical Association of America. Retrieved from http://www.maa.org/devlin/devlin_03_08.html

Duffy, F. (2002). *Step-up-to-excellence: An innovative approach to managing and rewarding performance in school systems*. Kent, England: Scarecrow Education.

Esteve, H. (2009, February 9). Governor offers to cut own pay, asks teachers to work for free. Retrieved from http://www.oregonlive.com/politics/index.ssf/2009/02/kulongoski_to_teachers_work_fo.html

Fasko, D. (2003). *Critical thinking and reasoning: Current research, theory and practice (Perspectives on creativity)*. Cresskill, NJ: Hampton Press.

Franklin, J., Sheridan, M., Achenbach, J., Stein, R., Spencer, H., & Spencer S. (2010, February 27). 8.8 magnitude earthquake hits central Chile. *The Washington Post*. Retrieved from http://www.washingtonpost.com/wp-dyn/content/article/2010/02/27/AR2010022700229.html

Gardner, H. (2008). *Five minds for the future*. Boston, MA: Harvard Business School Press. pp. xix, 142, 161.

Gardner, H. (2009). The five minds for the future: Cultivating and integrating new ways of thinking to empower the education enterprise. *American Association of School Administrators, 66*(2), 1–11.

Gladwell, M. (2002). *The tipping point: How little things can make a big difference*. New York: Little, Brown. pp. 9, 258, 259.

Gladwell, M. (2008). *Outliers: The story of success*. New York: Little, Brown.

Gladwell, M. (2009a). *What the dog saw*. New York: Little, Brown.

Gladwell, M. (2009b, July 28). Speech at the National Education Computing Conference in Washington, D.C.

Gladwell, M. (2010, February 10). What's inside the four walls of education? Speech presented at the American Association of School Administrators conference in Phoenix, AZ.

Gleick, J. (2008). *Chaos: Making a new science*. New York: Penguin Books.

Gowers, T. (2002). *Mathematics*. Toronto: Sterling Publishing.

Graham, S., & Hebert, M. (2010). *Writing to read: Evidence for how writing can improve reading*. Washington, DC: Alliance for Excellent Education.

Gregg, L. (2010). *Power strategies for response to intervention*. Englewood, CO: Lead + Learn Press. pp. 9, 21, 79.

Gregory, G. H., & Kuzmich, L. (2005a). *Differentiated literacy strategies: For student growth and achievement in grades K–6.* Thousand Oaks, CA: Corwin Press.

Gregory, G. H., & Kuzmich, L. (2005b). *Differentiated literacy strategies: For student growth and achievement in grades 7–12.* Thousand Oaks, CA: Corwin Press.

Grunwald, L., & Adler, S. J. (Eds.). (1999). *Letters of the Century: America 1900–1999.* New York: Dial Press.

Grunwald, M. (2009). Ben Bernanke: The 2009 Time person of the year. *Time, 174*(25), 44–78.

Gupta, S. (2010, March 8). Stopping hospital infections. Video interview with Peter Pronovost. Retrieved from http://www.nytimes.com/2010/03/09/science/09conv.html

Hattie, J. (2009). *Visible learning: A synthesis of over 800 meta-analyses relating to achievement.* New York: Routledge. pp. 28–29.

Haughey, D. (2010). SMART goals. Project SMART CO, UK. Retrieved from www.projectsmart.co.uk/pdf/smart-goals.pdf

Hazen, R. M., & Trefil, J. (2009). *Science matters: Achieving scientific literacy.* New York: Random House.

Henriquez, A. (2009, November 19). Improving the literacy skills of children and young adults. Testimony submitted to the House Committee on Education and Labor: Early Childhood, Elementary and Secondary Education Subcommittee. Washington, DC: Government Printing Office.

Hirsch, E. D., Jr. (1988). *Cultural literacy: What every American needs to know.* New York: Random House.

Hoffman, J. V., & Goodman, Y. (2009). *Changing literacies for changing times: An historical perspective on the future of reading research, public policy, and classroom practices.* New York: Routledge. pp. 98–99.

Houston, P. D., Blankenstein, A. M., & Cole, R. W. (2009). *Leaders as communicators and diplomats: The soul of educational leadership.* Thousand Oaks, CA: Sage Company.

Hyerle, D. (1988). *Eight visual tools: Thinking maps.* Cary, NC: Thinking Maps Press.

Hyerle, D. (2004). *Student successes with thinking maps: School-based research results, and models for achievement using visual tools.* Thousand Oaks, CA: Corwin Press.

Hyerle, D. (2009). *Visual tools for transforming information into knowledge.* 2nd ed. Thousand Oaks, CA: Corwin Press.

International Reading Association. (2008, October). Literacy facts compiled by ProLiteracy Worldwide and Alliance for Excellent Education. www.proliteracy.org

International Society for Technology in Education. (2009). National educational technology standards and performance indicators for administrators. Retrieved from www.iste.org/Content/NavigationMenu/NETS/ForAdministrators/2009Standards/NETS_for_Administrators_2009.htm

Jacobs, H. H. (2010). *Curriculum 21: Essential education for a changing world.* Alexandria, VA: Association For Supervision and Curriculum Development. pp. 102, 140–141.

Kurzweil, R. (2005). *The singularity is near: When humans transcend biology.* New York: Penguin Group.

Langer, J. A. (1995). *Envisioning literature.* New York: Teachers College Press.

Lapp, D., Flood, J., Heath, S. B., & Langer, J. (2009). The communicative, visual, and performative arts: Core components of literacy education. In A. Hoffman, V. James and Y. Goodman (Eds.), *Changing literacies for changing times: An historical perspective on the future of reading research, public policy, and classroom practice* (pp. 3–16). New York: Routledge.

Lavignac, A. (1922). *Musical education.* (Esther Singleton, Trans.). New York: Appleton and Company. (Original work published 1903).

Lockhart, P. (2002). A mathematician's lament. Retrieved from www.maa.org/devlin/LockhartsLament.pdf

Lorenz, E. (1961). The Butterfly Effect. Retrieved from http://www.aps.org/publications/apsnews/200301/history.cfm

Marshall, E. (2009, June 23). 12 rescued from Shenandoah River. *The Martinsburg Journal.* Retrieved from www.journal-news.net/page/content.detail/id/521335.html?nav=5006

Marzano, R. J. (2003). *What works in schools: Translating research into action.* Alexandria, VA: Association for Supervision and Curriculum Development.

Marzano, R. J., & Kendall, J. S. (2007). *The new taxonomy of educational objectives.* 2nd ed. Thousand Oaks, CA: Corwin Press.

McFadden, R. D. (2010, February 16). Times reporter held by Taliban is among Polk Award winners. *The New York Times.* Retrieved from www.nytimes.com/2010/02/16/nyregion/16polk.html?pagewanted=print

McKeown, M. G., Beck, I. L., & Blake, R. G. (2009). Rethinking reading comprehension instruction: A comparison of instruction for strategies and content approaches. *Reading Research Quarterly, 44*(3), 218–253.

Meyer, J., & Nicholas, P. (2009, December 29). Obama: U.S. is fighting back. *The Tribune Newspapers*, p. A1. Retrieved from www.chicagotribune.com/news/chi-tc-nw-plane-terror-1228-1229dec29,0,2178797.story

Moore, P. (2006). *Little book of big ideas: Science.* London, England: Elwin Street Limited.

Morrow, E. R. (Interviewer) & Robinson, J. (Interviewee). (1952). Free Minds and Hearts at Work [Interview transcript]. Retrieved from National Public Radio This I Believe site: http://thisibelieve.org/essays/featured/

National Council of Teachers of English. (2008). A statement on an education issue Approved by the NCTE Board of Directors and NCTE Executive Committee: The NCTE definition of 21st century literacies. Urbana, IL: National Council of Teachers of English.

National Council of Teachers of English. (2009). Standards for the assessment of reading and writing, revised edition. Retrieved from http://www.ncte.org/standards/assessmentstandards

National Reading Panel. (2000, December). Report of the National Reading Panel: Teaching children to read: An evidence-based assessment of the scientific research literature on reading and its implications for reading instruction. Jessup, MD: National Institute for Literacy. edpubs@inet.ed.gov

No Child Left Behind Act of 2001. Public Law 107-110, January 8, 2002, 115 STAT. 1425 (2002). (Congressional Record, Vol. 147 [2001]). Washington, DC: U.S. Government Printing Office.

Overbaugh, R., & Schultz, L. (2009, January 4). Bloom's taxonomy. Retrieved from www.medschool.vcu.edu/graduate/pgmdir_res/documents/bloomtaxonomy.pdf

Palevsky, M. (2009, April 17). Citizen journalist publishing standards. *Huffington Post.* Retrieved from www.huffingtonpost.com/2009/04/14/citizen-journalism-publis_n_186963.html

Partnership for 21st Century Skills. (2009). P-21 framework outcomes—Interdisciplinary themes for core subjects. Retrieved from www.p21.org/index.php?option=com_content&task=view&id=254&Itemid=120

Paulos, J. A. (1995). *A mathematician reads the newspaper.* New York: Random House.

Piercy, T. D. (2006). *Compelling conversations: Connecting leadership to student achievement.* Englewood, CO: Lead + Learn Press.

Piercy, T. D., & Piercy, W. J. (2003). Chaos in the classroom. In D. Fasko, Jr. (Ed.), *Critical thinking and reasoning: Current research, theory, and practice* (pp. 187–205). Cresskill, NJ: Hampton Press.

Pink, D. (2009). *Drive.* New York: Riverhead Books.

ProLiteracy. (2010). The impact of literacy. Retrieved from www.proliteracy.org/NetCommunity/Page.aspx?pid=345

Reeves, D. B. (2009). *Leading change in your school: How to conquer myths, build commitment, and get results.* Alexandria, VA: Association for Supervision and Curriculum Development.

Reeves, D. B. (2010). A framework for assessing 21st century skills. In J. Bellanca and R. Brandt (Eds.), *21st century skills: Rethinking how students learn* (pp. 305–326). Bloomington, IN: Solution Tree.

Robb, L., Klemp, R., & Schwartz, W. (2002). *Reader's handbook: A student guide for reading and learning.* Wilmington, MA: Great Source Education Group.

Roig-Franzia, M. (2010, January, 17). As lives and houses shattered in Haiti quake, so did some religious differences. Retrieved from www.washingtonpost.com/wp-dyn/content/article/2010/01/16/AR2010011603140.html?wprss=rss_print/asection

Routman, R. (2003). *Reading essentials: The specifics you need to teach reading well.* Portsmouth, NH: Heinemann.

Routman, R. (2010, April 15). State of Maryland International Reading Association conference address, Hunt Valley, Baltimore, MD.

Schlechty, P. C. (2009). *Leading for learning: How to transform schools into learning organizations.* San Francisco, CA: Jossey-Bass. p. 16.

Senge, P. M. (1990). *The fifth discipline: The art and practice of the learning organization.* New York: Doubleday Currency. p. 11.

Shanahan, T. (2009, December 10). You want to get it right, but it is so hard with so many different experts and so many different opinions. What is the right answer? Message posted to www.shananhan@uic.educ.

Shanahan, T., & Shanahan, C. (2008). Teaching disciplinary literacy to adolescents: Rethinking content. *Harvard Educational Review, 78*(1), 40–59.

Snow, C., & Moje, E. (2010). Why is everyone talking adolescent literacy? *Phi Delta Kappan, 91*(6), 66–69.

Solzhenitsyn, A. (1970). Nobel laureate acceptance speech for literature. Stockholm, Sweden. Retrieved from www.nobelprize.org/nobel_prizes/literature/laureates/1970/solzhenitsyn-lecture.html

Spurgin, T. (2009). The art of reading, lecture 4. The great courses. Chantilly, VA: The Teaching Company.

Stelter, B. (2010, February 21). Honoring citizen journalists. *The New York Times.* Retrieved from www.nytimes.com/2010/02/22/business/media/22polk.html?scp=1&sq=George%20Polk%20Award%202010%20%22February%2021%202010%22&st=cse

Todd, C. (Producer). (2008, December 8). Did you know: Campaign politics and the Internet. Washington, DC: CSPAN Broadcasting.

United States Department of Education. (2010a, March). A blueprint for reform: The reauthorization of the Elementary and Secondary Education Act. Washington, DC: U.S. Government Printing Office. edpubs@inet.ed.gov.

United States Department of Education. (2010b, March 29). Race to the top. USDE Office of Elementary and Secondary Education Publication No. CFDA Number: 84.395A. Washington, DC: U.S. Government Printing Office.

Universal Thesaurus online. (2009). www.universalthesaurus.com

Vacca, R. T., & Vacca, J. L. (1999). *Content area reading literacy and learning across the curriculum.* New York: Addison-Wesley Educational Publishers.

Webster's Online Dictionary. (2010). www.websters-online-dictionary.org

White, S. H. (2009). *Leadership maps.* Englewood, CO: Lead + Learn Press. pp. 138–150.

Whitecotton, B. (2010, April 10). Personal communication.

Wiggins, G., & McTighe, J. (2007). *Schooling by design: Mission, action, and achievement.* Alexandria, VA: Association for Supervision and Curriculum Development.

Wineburg, S. (2001). *Historical thinking and other unnatural acts: Charting the future of teaching the past.* Philadelphia, PA: Temple University Press.

Wineburg, S. (2007, June 5). Opening up the textbook and offering students a "second voice." *Education Week,* p. 23.

Wolf, M., & Barzillai, M. (2009, March). The best of both literacies. *Educational Leadership, 66*(6), 38–41.

Index